C. S. LEWIS:
A SHORT INTRODUCTION

Continuum Icons

Great books never go out of style, but they can go out of print. The Icons series is an attractively packaged collection of the greatest works of well-known authors. Enjoy them for the first time, or take some time to reacquaint yourself with these wonderful writers.

Books in the series include:

C. S. Lewis:
A Short Introduction

Philip Vander Elst

continuum
LONDON • NEW YORK

Continuum

The Tower Building, 11 York Road, London SE1 7NX
15 East 26th Street, New York NY 10010

www.continuumbooks.com

First published 1996 by The Claridge Press
This edition published in 2005 by Continuum

British Library Cataloguing-in-Publication Data
A catalogue record for this book is available from the British Library.

ISBN: 0-8264-8470-0

Printed and bound in Great Britain by Antony Rowe Ltd,
Chippenham, Wilts

CONTENTS

CONTENTS

1. C. S. Lewis — The Man and His Significance

On his death in 1963, the *Times Obituary* on C. S. Lewis described him as one of "the great lay preachers of our time". "As a Christian writer his influence was marked... he made religious books best-sellers and, in a nice sense, fashionable". Today, thirty years later, the popularity of C. S. Lewis's works has, if anything, grown. Despite Lewis's own pessimistic prediction that no one would read his books after he had been dead five or six years, nearly everything he wrote is still in print, much of it available in several languages, "and his works", according to one American scholar, Professor Lyle Dorsett, "sell better today than during his lifetime." Not only do his own writings sell extremely well, but — adds Professor Dorsett — "books about C. S. Lewis find a ready market too. Indeed, since his death almost 60 books have been written and edited on Lewis's life and work, hundreds of magazine and journal articles have appeared, and almost one hundred and fifty master's and doctoral dissertations have been prepared on this author".

Who, then, was C. S. Lewis? What sort of man was he, and what were the influences and forces that shaped him? Why, above all, did he make such an impact in his generation and what is his significance today?

A short introductory book like this one cannot hope to do more than skim the surface of his life and thought, but despite his prolific output and many-sided genius, the main elements of C. S. Lewis's life and work stand out very clearly.

He was born on 29 November 1898, near the outskirts of Belfast, the son of prosperous and well educated middle class parents. "Of his arrival", wrote his elder brother, Warren, who was three at the time, "I remember nothing, though no doubt I was introduced to him, and it was only by degrees that I became dimly conscious of him as a vociferous disturber of my domestic peace". Lewis, on his part, regarded his brother Warren as one of the blessings of his early years: "Though three years my senior, he never seemed to be an elder brother; we were allies, not to say confederates from the first".

His friendship with his brother, which lasted throughout his life, was but one of the blessings of his happy childhood, early "golden years" — as Lewis described them — characterised by such delights as those of rail travel each summer to and from nearby seaside resorts: "...the selection of toys to be taken, the bustle of packing, and then the great moment when the cab arrived to take us to the station. Then came the glorious excitement of the train journey, and, supreme bliss, the first sight of the sea." Other delights included the beautiful rolling country-side of Co. Down and the huge ramshackle Edwardian house into which the family moved in 1905, and which C. S. Lewis called "almost a major character in my story". As he put it in his autobiography, *Surprised by Joy*, "I am a product of long corridors, empty sunlit rooms, upstair indoor silences, attics explored in solitude, distant noises of gurgling cisterns and pipes, and the noise of wind under the tiles" — recollections woven into one of his famous Narnian chronicles, *The Magician's Nephew*.

The happy combination of country walks and bike rides, educated parents (his father was considered one of the best speakers in the Belmont Literary Society, and his mother was a brilliant mathematician and logician), and life in a fascinating and spacious house crammed full of books, imparted to the young C. S. Lewis an intense love of reading and offered every stimulus to the development of his enormous natural gifts of creativity and intelligence. It was in those early years in particular that he first heard "the horns of elfland" and acquired that passionate love of fantasy, fairy tale, myth and legend — or what he later called "Romance" — which so dominated his adult life and work. The impact natural scenery made on his imagination can be gauged from an essay he wrote 'On Stories' in 1947, in which he declares: "I have seen landscapes (notably in the Mourne Mountains) which, under a particular light, made me feel that at any moment a giant might raise his head over the next ridge. Nature has that in her which compels us to invent giants: and only giants will do".

In his tenth year, the golden landscape of Lewis's childhood was tragically overcast by the Shadow of Death — by the loss, through cancer, of the mother he dearly loved. "With my mother's death all settled happiness, all that was tranquil and reliable, disappeared from my life. There was to be much fun, many pleasures, many stabs of Joy; but no more of the old security. It was sea and islands now; the great continent had sunk like Atlantis."

The sudden and unexpected blow of his mother's death, like the introduction of a new and sombre movement in a symphony, inevitably darkened Lewis's outlook on the world, a process subsequently reinforced by his unhappy experience of boarding school — first at a prep school in Hertfordshire (which he called "Belsen", and whose cruel headmaster was eventually certified as insane) and then at Malvern, at that time (1913-14) a traditional public school whose whole life and ethos was typically uncongenial to a bookish intellectual like Lewis, who had no interest in or aptitude for 'games' (i.e. sport).

As he stated many years later, in an address given to the undergraduates of Magdalen College, Oxford, during the Second World War: "Perhaps because I had a not very happy boyhood... I am too familiar with the idea of futility to feel the shock of it so sharply as a good speaker on the subject ought to". Familiarity, in fact, with the idea of futility and the notion that we are alone in an indifferent or even hostile Universe, both contributed to the development of Lewis's own atheistic views as a young man, and enabled him — through personal experience and imaginative sympathy — to understand the outlook and emotions of the unbelieving and irreligious audiences who were the targets of his subsequent apologetic writings in defence of theism and Christianity.

Lewis's unhappy memories of boarding school life, especially his experience of bullying and persecution, also taught him to distrust what he would later recognise as 'fallen' human nature, and opened his eyes to the perils and problems of power — in particular, to the corrupting effects on human character of the 'worldly' desire to be 'on the inside', 'in the know', part of some 'inner ring' — an appetite fed by pride and snobbery, and which he fiercely denounced in later life. As he put it in an unpublished article criticising the naive views of Professor Haldane, a famous British scientist and Marxist of the 1940s, who thought capitalism was the root of all evil: "The difference between us is that the

Professor sees the 'world' purely in terms of those threats and those allurements which depend on money. I do not. The most 'worldly' society I have ever lived in is that of schoolboys: most worldly in the cruelty and arrogance of the strong, the toadyism and mutual treachery of the weak, and the unqualified snobbery of both. Nothing was so base that most members of the school proletariat would not do it, or suffer it, to win the favour of the school aristocracy: hardly any injustice too bad for the aristocracy to practice. But the class system did not in the least depend on the amount of anyone's pocket money. Who needs to care about money if most of the things he wants will be offered by cringing servility and the remainder can be taken by force? This lesson has remained with me all my life. That is one of the reasons why I cannot share Professor Haldane's exaltation at the banishment of Mammon from 'a sixth of our planet's surface' [the Soviet Union!]. I have already lived in a world from which Mammon was banished: it was the most wicked and miserable I have yet known." ('A Reply to Professor Haldane', *Of Other Worlds: Essays and Stories*, p.79).

Aware of his younger son's unhappiness at Malvern, his father, Albert — having consulted Lewis's elder brother, who had gone on to Sandhurst to begin a military career — withdrew him from school after the summer term of 1914 and entrusted him to a private tutor, William T Kirkpatrick, the former headmaster of Albert's old school, Lurgan College, in Co. Armagh, and a brilliant teacher.

Lewis's three years under the tutelage of Kirkpatrick, known affectionately as 'Kirk' are lovingly portrayed in his autobiography, *Surprised by Joy*, in which he describes life in 'Kirk's' beautiful house in Surrey and, more importantly, the impact his tutor made on his own mental development. This, apart from induction into a wide-ranging course of literary, classical and historical studies, chiefly consisted in the acquisition of a rigorous logical mind, moulded and stretched by debate and argument. "If ever a man came near to being a purely logical entity," said Lewis, "that man was Kirk... The most casual remark was taken as a summons to disputation." "To me," he wrote, "it was red beef and strong beer," and his own biographers and friends, Roger Lancelyn Green and Walter Hooper, comment: "this became his own method of argument, his own idea of conversation throughout his life. Who among his friends cannot still see him swing round with the light of good-humoured battle in his eyes on spotting a loose or too casual pronouncement, and hear his exultant cry of 'I challenge that!'?" (*C. S. Lewis: A Biography*).

The other principal result of Lewis's years with Kirkpatrick, who was a staunch rationalist and atheist, was the development and crystallisation of his own reasons for rejecting Christianity — aided by assiduous reading of the Rationalist Press Association pamphlets which littered Kirkpatrick's Surrey home. Lewis describes in detail the story of his apostasy and subsequent reconversion to Christianity in *Surprised by Joy*, and, allegorically, in his book, *The Pilgrim's Regress*, but the main point to make here is that his rejection of Christianity was not only fuelled by a dismaying awareness of the cruelty of the world and the fragility of human life and happiness, but was greatly influenced by his conviction that the central affirmation of Christianity — that God came down to Earth and became Man, and that His subsequent death and resurrection brought 'salvation' and new life to the human race — could be explained away (and therefore rejected) as but one of the many extant myths about a dying god who comes to life again, which can be found in numerous Pagan religions. This sceptical anthropological approach to the Christian story was not only stimulated by Lewis's extensive reading of myths and legends, but also by two contemporary critical works: Andrew Lang's *Myth, Ritual and Religion*, and Sir James Frazer's *The Golden Bough*. Hence his comment in a letter to his lifelong friend, Arthur Greaves, (12 October 1916) that "All religions, that is all mythologies, to give them their proper name, are merely man's own invention — Christ as much as Loki".

Two months after this letter to Greaves, Lewis went to Oxford to sit for a scholarship examination as the first step in what he, his father and his tutor hoped would become an academic career as an Oxford don — the future best fitted for someone of his temperament, ability and interests. It was also agreed that if he passed into Oxford, he would be able to join the Officers' Training Corps and get a commission as soon as his papers came through — for Lewis was determined to serve his country during the First World War even though, being Irish born, he was exempt from conscription.

Lewis duly succeeded in becoming a scholar of University College, and after a brief interruption of his Oxford career caused by his wartime service in France from November 1917 to April 1918 — when he was wounded during the Battle of Arras and sent home with a fragment of shell lodged in his chest — resumed his studies in January 1919, eventually gaining a triple First in English and Classics (including Philosophy), and becoming a Fellow of Magdalen College in September 1925.

It was during his years as a young Oxford don, as a Tutor in English Language and Literature, that C. S. Lewis developed some of his closest lifelong friendships — principally with such future giants of the English academic and literary world as Tolkien and Neville Coghill, and, in later years, Charles Williams, Dorothy Sayers and Roger Lancelyn Green (a former pupil of his). But the most important event of Lewis's life in the 1920s, the one which transformed his work and career, was his conversion to Christianity in 1929.

Although, for reasons already alluded to, Lewis had definitely turned away from Christianity in his teens (only allowing himself to be 'confirmed' into the Church of England to avoid upsetting his father), his tastes, wrote Professor Coghill in 1965, "were essentially for what had magnitude and a suggestion of myth: the heroic and romantic never failed to excite his imagination, and although at that time he was something of a professed atheist, the mystically supernatural things in ancient epic and saga always attracted him." (*C. S. Lewis: A Biography*). In particular, he was haunted throughout his early life by what he called "Joy", or "the inconsolable longing", an experience of beauty, sweetness, and rapture which came to him through specific passages in literature and music, or through a landscape, but could not be located in or identified with them. As Lewis wrote some years later: "...it [the beauty] was not *in* them, it only came *through* them, and what came through them was longing... For they are not the thing itself; they are only the scent of a flower we have not found, the echo of a tune we have not heard, news from a country we have never yet visited." (*Transposition and Other Addresses*, chapter 2). As he put it even more vividly in his autobiography: "Joy itself, considered simply as an event in my own mind, turned out to be of no value at all. All the value lay in that of which Joy was the desiring. And that object, quite clearly, was no state of my own mind or body at all... Inexorably Joy proclaimed, 'You want — I myself am your want of — something other, outside, not you or any state of you.' I did not yet ask, Who is the desired? only What is it?

But this brought me already into the region of awe, for I thus understood that in deepest solitude there is a road right out of the self, a commerce with something which, by refusing to identify itself with any object of the senses, or anything whereof we have biological or social need, or anything imagined, or any state of our own minds, proclaims itself sheerly objective. Far more objective than bodies, for it is not, like them, clothed in our senses; the naked Other, imageless (though our imagination salutes it with a hundred images), unknown, undefined, desired."

This recurrent experience of the "inconsolable longing", which Lewis later recognised had its source in God — that "naked Other" proclaiming "itself sheerly objective" — kept the door of his mind open to the possibility that Christianity might, after all, be true, a possibility reinforced by conversations with Christian friends like Tolkien and Hugo Dyson, who helped him to see that his dismissal of Christianity on the grounds that the story of Jesus merely echoed Pagan myths about dying gods, could be turned on its head: their similarity to central aspects of the Gospel could just as easily be regarded as evidence in favour of the truth of Christianity, as dreams or premonitions of God's redemptive work through Christ. To put it in Lewis's words: "The Divine light, we are told, 'lighteneth every man'. We should, therefore, expect to find in the imagination of great Pagan teachers and myth-makers some glimpse of that theme which we believe to be the very plot of the whole cosmic story — the theme of incarnation, death and rebirth." At the time that this possibility first dawned on him, however, it came as a shock. Hence Lewis describes how he was shattered, on one occasion in 1926, when the hardest-boiled atheist he knew not only remarked on what good evidence there was for the historicity of the Gospels, but added: "Rum thing. All that stuff of Frazer's about the Dying God. Rum thing. It almost looks as if it had really happened once."

The most interesting feature of C. S. Lewis's conversion to Christianity was that it was involuntary. As is clear from his own writings, autobiographical and apologetic, he did not relish the prospect of encountering God as Absolute Goodness, the Omniscient and Omnipotent Creator ("King" and "Hunter") whose Holiness will not abide or tolerate sin, and whose Love is remorselessly determined to remove that sin and change us into His image at whatever cost to us or to Him. Hence Lewis's comment that "the notion that everyone would *like* Christianity to be true, and therefore all atheists are brave men who have accepted the defeat of all their deepest desires, is simply impudent nonsense." In *his* case, he describes, in the most famous passage of his autobiography, his final reluctant surrender to God in the following words:

"You must picture me alone in that room in Magdalen, night after night, feeling, whenever my mind lifted even for a second from my work, the steady, unrelenting approach of Him whom I so earnestly desired not to meet. That which I greatly feared had at last come upon me. In the Trinity Term of 1929 I gave in, and admitted that God was God, and knelt and prayed: perhaps, that night, the most dejected and reluctant convert in all England."

It was only later, and by degrees, that Lewis became aware, as he put it, of "the Divine humility which will accept a convert even on such terms," and as the years passed and his awareness of "the depth of the Divine mercy" grew, and with it, his understanding of Christianity and its links with all that he most loved and cherished in literature and life, so he finally came to see his conversion experience as a wonderful and joyous ambush by God — that 'Joy' by which he was eventually 'Surprised' and which he therefore used as the title and theme of his autobiography. This experience and understanding also led him, once he had become a world-famous, best-selling Christian author, to donate any money made from specifically religious writings to charities, since — to quote his words to his friend, Walter Hooper — "I felt that God had been so gracious in having me that the least I could do was give back all the money made in His service".

The period after his conversion, especially the 1940s — but continuing right up to his death in 1963, saw the full flowering of Lewis's genius as a Christian philosopher and apologist, a noted English scholar, and a hugely popular broadcaster, lecturer, and writer of fantasy and romance — from 'children's fairy tales' (to use a conventional but misleading label which he hated) to 'science fiction' (also, in Lewis's eyes, a narrow and misleading phrase).

Of his work and achievements as an English academic, this study can say little, since shortage of space and the need to do justice to his fiction and his popular theological writings precludes a detailed analysis, but the main thrust of his critical scholarship — and his chief claim to fame in the academic world — was to break down "the artificial barrier that had been erected by scholars and historians between the Middle Ages and the Renaissance". (*C. S. Lewis: A Biography.*) The fact that Cambridge subsequently established a new Chair of Medieval and Renaissance English for Lewis to fill in 1954, proved the extent of his success in this area. Lewis also became famous for his insistence on the continuity of English literature up to 1830, and its close connection with Christianity. More controversially, he also deplored what he saw as the harmful impact of humanism on English literature and thought from the sixteenth century onwards — meaning, by 'humanism', the notion that Man, not God, is the measure of all things and the central point of reference in art and philosophy. These, and many other insights, can be found in his best known academic works, *The Allegory of Love: A Study in Medieval Tradition* (1936); Volume III of *The Oxford History of English Literature — English Literature in the Sixteenth Century, Excluding Drama* (1954); and *The Discarded Image: An Introduction to Medieval and Renaissance Literature* (1964).

One of the connecting links between Lewis's outlook as a Christian apologist, a political and cultural 'conservative' and an English scholar, was his dislike of "chronological snobbery" — the growing insistence, which he detected and opposed during his lifetime, that what was new and modern was *ipso facto* better than what had gone before. Thus in *Surprised by Joy* he records with gratitude the debt he owed his friend Owen Barfield, who taught him to see through "the uncritical acceptance of the intellectual climate common to our own age and the assumption that whatever has gone out of date is on that account discredited. You must find out why it went out of date. Was it ever refuted (and if so by whom, where, and how conclusively) or did it merely die away as fashions do? If the latter, this tells us nothing about its truth or falsehood".

It was precisely this awareness of the pitfalls and defects of "chronological snobbery" that led Lewis to emphasise the critical importance of reading old as well as modern literature. In his preface to St. Athanasius's *The Incarnation of the Word of God*, a translation first published in 1944 by Geoffrey Bles, he declared: "Every age has its own outlook. It is specially good at seeing certain truths and specially liable to make certain mistakes. We all, therefore, need the books that will correct the characteristic mistakes of our own period. And that means the old books".

In other words, to quote Lewis, we need "to keep the clean sea breeze of the centuries blowing through our minds" in order to free ourselves from the intellectual provincialism of the present.

Lewis's own determination and ability to swim against the intellectual and cultural currents of the twentieth century are apparent in his works of popular theology and in his fictional 'romances'. In a succession of closely argued books, the principal ones being *Miracles* (1947), *Mere Christianity* (his famous wartime BBC broadcast talks published separately in the 1940s, and in this one volume in 1952), *The Problem of Pain* (1940), and *The Abolition of Man* (1943), C. S. Lewis sympathetically but systematically confronts and counters most of the principal attacks launched against Christianity by atheists, agnostics and other unbelievers, and then goes on to expound and defend the meaning and truth of the Christian Faith, and the saneness and rationality of the central tradition of Christian ethics and culture, in language which even his critics have always conceded combines a unique blend of logical rigour, clarity, and illuminating metaphor. In these and other books, articles, lectures and addresses, the open-minded reader will find a vigorous affirmation of the existence of God, the inner contradictions of atheism, the reality of miracles and the supernatural, the historicity of the Gospel, the objectivity of moral values, and the goodness of God. In them, too, he or she will find a lucid and unblushing exposition not only of such great traditional Christian doctrines as the Fall of Man, the Incarnation, the Atonement, and the Second Coming, but also — particularly in *The Screwtape Letters* (from an older to a younger devil, first published in 1942) — an often witty but always perceptive dissection of evil, pride, temptation and human frailty.

As is so often the case, Lewis's success as a popular writer and theologian in the 1940s and fifties did not endear himself to many of his, no doubt jealous, academic colleagues, but his impact on several generations of Oxford undergraduates can be gauged from the crowds who regularly attended his lectures and sermons, and from the equally well attended meetings of the Oxford University Socratic Club, founded, with Lewis as President, at the end of 1941. At these meetings, organised to encourage rational debate and discussion between Christians and non-Christians, papers would be given and counter-attacked by rival speakers, and C. S. Lewis's contributions never failed to arouse the greatest interest — sometimes attracting audiences of several hundred. The often humorous flavour of these discussions, despite the seriousness of the issues involved, emerges from the description given of one Socratic Club meeting in Roger Lancelyn Green's and Walter Hooper's biography of Lewis, published in 1974: "...many Socratic members will recall the evening on which the first speaker was a Relativist who was said to have ended his talk with the assertion: 'the world does not exist, England does not exist, Oxford does not exist, and I am confident that *I* do not exist!' When Lewis was asked to reply, he stood up and said, 'How am I to talk to a man who's *not there*?'"

Like Chesterton, whose books greatly influenced him, C. S. Lewis had a shrewd and humorous understanding of the 'common man', and this reinforced his capacity as a communicator to express Christian truth in language accessible to the uneducated layman. Two of his published essays, for instance, 'God In the Dock' (1948) and 'Christian Apologetics' (an address originally given to an assembly of Anglican priests and youth leaders in 1945) consist of a witty and penetrating account of the mentality of popular audiences, their knowledge of religion and history, and their understanding of Christian and religious vocabulary, and provide an amusing insight into Lewis's ability to build bridges between his own erudition and understanding and that of 'the man in the street'. Hooper and Green's biography of Lewis also records at least one example of Lewis's talent for face to face communication in the most unlikely situations: "Clifford Morris, whose taxi he had been accustomed to hire... whenever he needed transport... writes: 'I shall always consider myself fortunate to have been included in his circle of friendship... He was never an intellectual snob, and he was willing to talk to anyone on any subject... I have been with him in the company of Oxford and Cambridge professors, and I have overheard some of their conversation — conversation that I was totally unable to understand or share; and I have also been with him, sitting in the middle of a crowd of lorry drivers in a transport cafe, while he enthralled them with his wit and conversational powers. After one of these occasions one of the men came to me and said, 'Hey, mate, who's the guv'nor?' And when I told him, he expressed surprise, and then said, 'Blimey, he's a toff, he is! A real nice bloke!'"

Despite the brilliance and luminosity of Lewis's forays into popular philosophy and theology, some would argue that his chief claim to fame, and the field in which he has made the most lasting impact, has been as a writer of 'children's fiction' and as the author of the 'science fiction' trilogy: *Out of the Silent Planet* (1938), *Perelandra (Voyage to Venus)* (1943), and *That Hideous Strength* (1945). Whether or not this is really the case, it is certainly true that Lewis's fictional output (whose themes and ideas are explored in a separate chapter) not only displays a rich and powerful imagination, and abundant wit and charm, but once again reveals his profound understanding of the human condition and his unique talent for expressing Christian truths in hidden and unexpected guises which, by disarming readers' prejudices, allows these truths to appear fresh and original — free of their "stained glass and Sunday school associations". Hence the power and impact of the account, in *Voyage to Venus*, of the 'temptation of Eve', and of the 'creation narrative' in *The Magician's Nephew*.

It should, incidentally, be emphasised at this juncture, that Lewis himself constantly pointed out that none of the 'romances' making up his science fiction trilogy and *The Chronicles of Narnia* originated in any didactic purpose. He did not set out to convey a Christian message in fictional form, but would start out with "pictures" in his mind of characters or scenes around which he then wrote his stories — the Christian themes emerging later of their own accord. He also insisted that children, as readers, should neither be patronised nor idolised, hating the "professional attitude which regards children in the lump as a sort of raw material which we have to handle". As he put it in his essay 'On Three Ways of Writing for Children': "Once in a hotel dining-room I said, rather too loudly, 'I loathe prunes'. 'So do I', came an unexpected six-year old's voice from another table. Sympathy was instantaneous. Neither of us thought it funny. We both knew that prunes are far too nasty to be funny. That is the proper meeting between man and child as independent personalities. Of the far higher and more difficult relations between child and parent or child and teacher, I say nothing. An author, as a mere author, is outside all that. He is not even an uncle. He is a freeman and an equal, like the postman, the butcher, and the dog next door."

In recent years, C. S. Lewis has become known to a wider public not only through the (only partially successful) televising of *The Lion, The*

Witch, And the Wardrobe and *The Silver Chair*, but also via the dramatic representation of the story of his marriage (late in his life) to Joy Davidman, in *Shadowlands*, first produced for television, then as a West End play, and most recently as an award-winning film directed by Sir Richard Attenborough.

The fascinating and moving aspect of this event and period in Lewis's life, is not so much that he 'found love' and got married only a few years before his death, but that he fell in love with the most unlikely woman imaginable, and in the most extraordinary circumstances.

Joy Davidman was a talented New York poet, born of Jewish parents, a former atheist and Communist, divorced and 17 years younger than Lewis. She, and her first husband, had been converted to Christianity partly through reading Lewis's books, and she met him for the first time in September 1952 — when her first marriage was already disintegrating. Lewis found Joy a splendid intellectual companion and "they struck fire from one another" (to quote Green and Hooper) from the first moment they met, but Lewis only married her in April 1956 in a registry office wedding to prevent the Home Office deporting her and her two young sons, their permit to stay in England having been terminated with no reason given. Then, when Joy was dying of bone cancer in March 1957, a proper bedside marriage was celebrated in the Churchill Hospital at Oxford, partly because Joy did not want to die in hospital and Lewis felt he could not bring her to his home unless they were married in the sight of God as well as in the sight of man.

The sequel to these events — the story of Joy's miraculous but temporary recovery from cancer (the result, in both their eyes, of prayer) and the blossoming of their love — is movingly portrayed in *Shadowlands* and described in various biographies, as is the return of Joy's cancer, her death in July 1960, and C. S. Lewis's subsequent grief. What *Shadowlands* does not portray, however, is the manner in which Lewis wrestled with his sense of grief and loss — described in detail in his own book (a diary), *A Grief Observed*, first published under the pseudonym of N. W. Clerk in 1961. *Shadowlands* underlines his terrible sorrow and the challenge the loss of his wife posed to his faith in God, but fails to show the maturing and re-emergence of his Christian confidence and understanding at the end of the grieving process. It is, for instance, significant, that numerous friends, acquaintances and fans — unaware of the true authorship of *A Grief Observed*, and finding it a strong and ultimately comforting book — sent Lewis gift copies of his own work in the hope of consoling him! Viewers of *Shadowlands* who do not know C. S. Lewis's writings would also miss the fact that far from losing his faith as the play hints, Lewis subsequently wrote a powerful Christian classic, *Letters to Malcolm: Chiefly on Prayer*, published after his death, which was described by the *Church Times* as showing "the grasp of the reality of God, the determination to put truth before passing fashion, the apprehension of the mystery and the glory of grace," all of which helped "to make this book pure treasure".

What, to conclude, is the significance of C. S. Lewis? I hope that a full answer to that question will emerge in the subsequent chapters of this introductory study; but this much can already be said and was already obvious in his lifetime: his life and work not only challenges the prevailing assumption of modern, secularised intellectuals that Christianity is outmoded, irrational, gloomy and obscurantist; it is also the perfect antidote to that spirit of 'scientific' rationalism and humanism which has so dominated the twentieth century and which is incarnated in the works of men like Bertrand Russell, H. G. Wells, and their successors today.

2. The Repudiation of Atheism

Centuries ago the Book of *Ecclesiastes* (1:9) declared that "there is nothing new under the sun," and that is certainly true of the age-old philosophical debate about the existence of God. Although atheism is commonly conceived as the distinctive product and expression of the modern scientific age, it actually predates the rise of modern science by several millennia, originating with the Ancient Greeks. Theism, on the other hand, while equally ancient in origin, has been as closely associated with the scientific spirit as atheism. Not only have some of the greatest scientists in history been Christians — like Newton, Kepler, Faraday and Pasteur — but as one Christian philosopher and scientist, E. L. Mascall, pointed out in his 1956 Bampton lectures, *Christian Theology and Natural Science*, modern experimental science largely developed in the West because of the conviction that the Universe is the creation of a rational intelligence, and can therefore be systematically investigated to discover the 'laws' and processes by which it is governed. The existence of God was seen as a guarantee of the orderliness of Nature, and thus of the possibility of understanding her mechanisms and structure through observation and experiment.

Nevertheless, despite this central fact about the cultural soil from which science originally sprang, it is undoubtedly true that scepticism about the existence of God has dominated modern philosophical and scientific thought since the end of the nineteenth century, and it was especially strong in C. S. Lewis' generation — more so than today. The reasons for this are various, but four factors in particular account for the growth and prevalence of modern atheism, which Lewis embraced as a young man but eventually rejected at the end of the 1920s.

The first is the conviction, an article of faith with many, that the theory of evolution explains the origin and development of life in the Universe, and accounts for the appearance of design in Nature — fulfilling the role of a 'Blind Watchmaker' (to quote the title of Richard Dawkins' book on this subject), and thereby dispensing with the need to invoke the idea of God. Secondly, as the growth of scientific knowledge has increased our awareness of the immensity of the Universe, so our human sense of cosmic loneliness and insignificance has grown, and with it an increasing inability to believe that human life and the natural order reflect any transcendent purpose. This sense of the hugeness of the Cosmos and its indifference to Man, moreover, is also reinforced by our awareness of the problem of suffering and evil. This is an old stumbling block to belief in the existence of God, but one which has seemingly grown in size and sharpness as the horrors of totalitarianism and war in the 20th century have eclipsed 19th century optimism about the inevitability of progress. Finally, and not least important, the Judeo-Christian concept of God as the Creator and Redeemer of mankind is inherently distasteful to many people, especially intellectuals, since the idea that we owe our existence and should give our allegiance to some Divine Power behind the Universe, is hurtful to their pride and threatens their sense of independence, self-sufficiency and freedom. In particular, the Bible's affirmation that Man has sinned against God — has in some sense offended that Divine Power and needs redemption — is especially unwelcome to those who are satisfied with their characters and unaware of any deep-seated moral flaw about which they need to repent.

This is not, of course, to say that all atheist sentiment is distorted by wishful thinking, or that there are not honest and apparently powerful arguments for disbelieving in the existence of God. The point is simply that it is apparent from introspection, observation and experience that many who reject God are no freer from prejudice and mixed motives than their religious-minded opposites, and it is important to bear this in mind when looking afresh at the debate about God's existence and the ebb and flow of faith versus unbelief.

Growing up in the fresh self-confident climate of late Victorian and Edwardian rationalism, when Christianity looked increasingly timid, old-fashioned and unscientific, and belief in the existence and goodness of God was further undermined by the outbreak of the First World War,

C. S. Lewis initially developed an irreligious outlook similar in some respects to that of Bertrand Russell, who — with H. G. Wells — was perhaps the most popular, robust and influential apostle of twentieth century atheism. Given this fact, therefore, and the additional point that this brand of atheism states the case against God more clearly and forcefully than any other, it is the logical place at which to begin our examination of Lewis's journey from scepticism to theism.

In his book, *Mysticism and Logic*, Bertrand Russell declares "That Man is the product of causes which had no pre-vision of the end they were achieving; that his origin, his growth, his hopes and fears, his love and his beliefs, are but the outcome of accidental collocations of atoms; that no fire, no heroism, no intensity of thought and feeling, can preserve an individual life beyond the grave; that all the labours of the ages, all the devotion, all the inspiration, all the noonday brightness of human genius, are destined to extinction in the vast death of the solar system, and that the whole temple of Man's achievement must inevitably be buried beneath the debris of a universe in ruins — all these things, if not quite beyond dispute, are yet so nearly certain that no philosophy which rejects them can hope to stand. Only within the scaffolding of these truths, only on the firm foundation of unyielding despair, can the soul's habitation henceforth be safely built." Furthermore, argues Russell, in *What I Believe*, there is no evidence of the existence of an intelligent and benevolent Creator: "Would not a world of nightingales and larks and deer be better than our human world of cruelty and injustice and war?... If I were granted omnipotence, and millions of years to experiment in, I should not think Man much to boast of as the final result of all my efforts."

Russell's forthright pessimism, and his arguments against the existence of God and any benevolent purpose behind creation, were fully shared by C. S. Lewis in his pre-Christian days, as he revealed in the opening passages of *The Problem of Pain.* But as Lewis argued in more than one place, we cannot denounce the evils of the world and the injustices of life, or rebel against the apparent senselessness and cruelty of Nature, unless we believe that the moral standard by which we judge the realities which surround us is in some sense objective and well founded. Otherwise the argument that the existence of suffering and evil disproves the existence of God, collapses, since we cannot condemn God or reject the idea of His existence merely because the Universe does not happen to please our private and subjective fancies. If, however, our sense of right and wrong, good and evil, is justified and true, where does it come from? How do we account for the existence of conscience, and our awareness of what Lewis called the Moral Law? If the Universe we live in is full of pain, suffering and evil, and does not therefore correspond with our idea of goodness, does this not suggest that our minds and our sense of values must — in some sense — be the product or reflection of Something *outside*, or *beyond* the order of Nature?

To quote Lewis in *Mere Christianity*: "... in the very act of trying to prove that God did not exist — in other words, that the whole of reality was senseless — I found I was forced to assume that one part of reality — namely my idea of justice — was full of sense. Consequently atheism turns out to be too simple. If the whole universe has no meaning, we should never have found out that it has no meaning: just as, if there were no light in the universe and therefore no creatures with eyes, we should never know it was dark. *Dark* would be without meaning." (p.42)

Here we see one of the characteristic traits of C. S. Lewis's apologetics: his ability, as in judo, to turn the apparent strength of an opposing argument into a weapon against the position he is attacking.

However, despite the skill with which Lewis deploys the moral argument for the existence of God, it commonly encounters two related objections, both of which amount to an attempt to explain away our moral consciousness and remove the element of mystery about its conflict with our natural and social environment.

It is first of all argued that what we call 'Conscience' is in fact 'herd instinct', developed in the course of evolution to facilitate and maximise human co-operation and survival. Secondly, the apparently 'objective' character of moral consciousness has a perfectly obvious utilitarian explanation since it simply reflects the fact that adherence to moral rules prohibiting theft, murder, dishonesty, and other forms of anti-social behaviour, is necessary to the preservation and enhancement of human life. In other words, our recognition of the value of life, and the conditions in which it best flourishes, both explains and justifies our moral perceptions without any need to invoke the idea of God. Furthermore, the validity of this non-theistic explanation of our moral consciousness is reinforced by the observation — a favourite one of Bertrand Russell's

— that the moral codes of different societies, and of the same societies in different periods of history, vary greatly, suggesting that there isn't, after all, a universally perceived Moral Law whose existence must have a Divine origin.

This apparently common-sensical, scientific approach looks impressive at first sight, but as Lewis showed, its initial plausibility melts away on closer examination.

To begin with, our moral awareness cannot be identified with our instincts since our instincts are impulses which are frequently in conflict with each other whereas what needs to be explained is that sense of obligation, or duty, which tells us to follow one impulse rather than another.

> Supposing you hear a cry for help from a man in danger. You will probably feel two desires — one a desire to give help (due to your herd instinct), the other a desire to keep out of danger (due to the instinct for self-preservation). But you will find inside you, in addition to these two impulses, a third thing which tells you that you ought to follow the impulse to help, and suppress the impulse to run away. Now this thing that judges between two instincts, that decides which should be encouraged, cannot itself be either of them. You might as well say that the sheet of music which tells you, at a given moment, to play one note on the piano and not another, is itself one of the notes on the keyboard. The Moral Law tells us the tune we have to play: our instincts are merely the keys. (*Mere Christianity*, p20-21.)

Not only, then, is it wrong to regard our moral sense as an instinct or set of instincts, but it is equally implausible to argue that it reflects some evolutionary 'law of survival' which has produced a set of habits conducive to the wellbeing and convenience of the human race. In the first place, the Moral Law frequently tells us to do (or not do) things which conflict with our personal desires and interests.

"... you cannot say," wrote Lewis, "that what we call decent behaviour in others is simply the behaviour that happens to be useful to us," since we do not, for example, admire traitors however helpful they may be to our country or our cause. "And as for decent behaviour in ourselves, I suppose it is pretty obvious that it does not mean the behaviour that pays. It means things like being content with thirty shillings when you might have got three pounds, doing school work honestly when it would be easy to cheat, leaving a girl alone when you would like to make love to her, staying in dangerous places when you could go somewhere safer, keeping promises you would rather not keep, and telling the truth even when it makes you look a fool." (*Mere Christianity*, p.27)

Secondly, at the social level, it is simply untrue to equate moral norms — like justice and fairness — with the dictates of 'survival'. The deliberate arrest and imprisonment of an innocent man for a crime he did not commit, for instance, might in some circumstances be in the 'interest' of society if the provision of a scapegoat were the only way of averting serious public disorder in the wake of some economic or social calamity, but it would hardly be 'just' or 'deserved'. Furthermore, as history and daily experience testify, there is little connection between, on the one hand, 'survival' and 'success', and — on the other — what we usually understand by 'goodness'. Cunning, ruthlessness, dishonesty and violence are frequently the 'road to the top', as politicians, criminals and dictators have proved down the ages, and the 'survival of the fittest' has often led to the triumph of war over peace, barbarism over civilisation, and tyranny over liberty. As every news bulletin reminds us, the 'law of survival', whether in Bosnia or the Sudan, Iraq or South Africa, is often indistinguishable from the law of the jungle precisely because so much of the world we live in *is* a jungle — an arena of hatred, conflict, and passion, in which truth and virtue are handicaps to advancement.

For these reasons, it is absurd, as Lewis pointed out, to maintain that our moral consciousness is somehow the product of some Darwinian process of 'natural selection':

> Anyone studying Man from the outside as we study electricity or cabbages, not knowing our language and consequently not able to get any inside knowledge from us, but merely observing what we did, would never get the slightest evidence that we had this moral law. How could he? For his observations would only show what we did, and the moral law is about what we ought to do. (*Mere Christianity*, p.31)

But, it may be objected, the sad fact that human beings too often behave badly and irrationally does not alter the truth that respect for moral norms and rules is in everyone's long-term interest, since it is vital to the achievement of happiness, order and progress for humanity as a whole. Hence the secular utilitarian interpretation of morality remains valid and is not undermined by the weakness of Darwinian arguments.

Unfortunately, as Lewis demonstrated, this attempt to provide a humanistic basis for ethics, without reference to God, still fails to stand the test of rigorous analysis. It involves a circular process of reasoning whose premise already assumes the truth of the conclusion it is trying to prove — namely: that human life is precious and we ought therefore to respect the rights and interests of others:

> ... of course, it is perfectly true that safety and happiness can only come from individuals, classes, and nations being honest and fair and kind to each other. It is one of the most important truths in the world. But as an explanation of why we feel as we do about Right and Wrong it just misses the point. If we ask: 'Why ought I to be unselfish?' and you reply 'Because it is good for society', we may then ask, 'Why should I care what's good for society except when it happens to pay *me* personally?' and then you will have to say, 'Because you ought to be unselfish' — which simply brings us back to where we started. (*Mere Christianity*, p.28)

Humanistic utilitarians, wrote Lewis, are similarly mistaken in their belief that the existence of a universal Moral Law rooted in God is disproved by the variations and changes that have occurred in the moral codes of different ages and societies. For a start, the differences that can be found are more apparent than real. Either they tend to reflect variations of belief about particular *facts* (such as whether witchcraft exists and therefore should be punished), or they reveal different degrees of insight about the *application* or *ramifications* of particular moral norms (such as whether kindness should be shown towards animals as well as children). They do not, in the main, reveal any real disagreement about the great moral platitudes which tell us not to murder, lie, or steal, or which remind us of our duties to our families and neighbours, and tell us that kindness, love and fairness are better than cruelty, hatred, and injustice.

Pointing out the similarities between the moral codes of the ancient Egyptians, Babylonians, Hindus, Chinese, Greeks and Romans, Lewis adds:

> I need only ask the reader to think what a totally different morality
> would mean. Think of a country where people were admired for run-
> ning away in battle, or where a man felt proud of double-crossing all
> the people who had been kindest to him. You might just as well try to
> imagine a country where two and two made five. (*Mere Christianity*,
> p.17)

Not only is it implausible to deny the existence of a universal moral
consciousness, but the very idea of 'progress', so dear to modern secu-
larists and humanists, logically implies the existence of an unchanging
moral standard against which we can compare different ages and societies, and determine whether or not there has been any moral 'advance'
over a particular period or in a given set of laws and institutions.

> Our ideas of the good may change, but they cannot change either for
> the better or the worse if there is no absolute and immutable good to
> which they can approximate or from which they can recede. We can
> go on getting a sum more and more nearly right only if the one per-
> fectly right answer is 'stagnant'... ('The Poison of Subjectivism', in
> *Christian Reflections*, p. 76.)

What this whole train of reasoning implies for the debate surrounding
the moral argument for the existence of God, said Lewis, is that ultimately there are only two ways of looking at moral values. They are
either an expression and rationalisation of our feelings and emotions,
with no claim to objectivity or truth, or their truth must be taken to be
self-evident, failure to grasp them being the moral equivalent of colour
blindness.

If the nihilists and sceptics are right in thinking that morality is an
illusion, the proven existence of a universal moral consciousness must
be regarded as a strange quirk of the human mind, an inexplicable mystery of the human spirit. If, on the other hand, our consciousness of
moral obligation is not illusory, but "a message from the core of reality," we have to face the fact that the conflict between the Moral Law
and actual human conduct, between our sense of values and the world in
which we live, suggests that our moral sense is not 'man-made' or "a

product of non-moral, non-rational Nature," but "an offshoot of some absolute moral wisdom" which is self-existent and therefore Divine. Hence C. S. Lewis's insistence that "the defiance of the good atheist hurled at an apparently ruthless and idiotic cosmos is really an unconscious homage to something in or behind that cosmos which he recognises as infinitely valuable and authoritative". ('De Futilitate', in *Christian Reflections*, p. 70.)

Those (let us hope the majority) who regard their moral judgements as something more than an expression of personal preference, on a par with their liking for ice-cream, may find the moral argument for the existence of God persuasive. But what should be the response to the philosophical sceptic who sticks to his guns, maintaining that morality is indeed an illusion, unembarrassed by his inability to provide any credible explanation for the existence of this extraordinary fiction?

Here we encounter one of the most important (and famous) of all C.S. Lewis's arguments against atheism: namely, that it cuts its own throat because its mechanistic explanation of the origin of life and human consciousness discredits all human knowledge and reasoning — including the arguments for atheism.

The kernel of Lewis's epistemological case against atheism and philosophical scepticism can be stated in brief and simple terms.

All philosophical debate — whether about the existence of God or anything else — necessarily involves a process of argument and therefore has to assume the validity of logical reasoning, that is to say, it assumes that when we draw a logical inference from a particular premise to a particular conclusion (e.g. if $A = B$, and $B = C$, it follows that $A = C$), we are reasoning 'correctly' in the sense of reaching or expressing a genuine 'truth'. Our knowledge of the Universe similarly depends on assuming the validity of logical inference (e.g. I know there is someone else in my office *because* he is coming towards me with a file and is speaking to me). To deny all this would involve the self-contradictory notion that 'we *know* that we cannot know anything', which is like saying: 'I can *prove* that there are no such things as proofs' — an obviously nonsensical statement. It consequently follows that any philosophical theory which discredits the possibility of knowledge and, as a result, our moral and religious perceptions, is self-refuting because it undermines its own intellectual credentials. This, however, is effectively what atheism does.

By saying that the Universe (or Nature) is all that exists, and that all human and animal life, and all structures, are simply the accidental and unintended product of blind physical and chemical processes, atheism (or 'naturalism') necessarily discredits all human reasoning since, as Lewis wrote in the first edition of his famous book, *Miracles*, no thought can be shown to be valid "if it can be fully explained as the result of irrational causes." But if it is really the case that we cannot trust our reasoning and therefore be confident of the truthfulness of any of our conclusions, atheists have no grounds for denying the existence of God since their own minds and thoughts are *also* the result of irrational causes: "If minds are wholly dependent on brains, and brains on bio-chemistry, and bio-chemistry (in the long run) on the meaningless flux of atoms, I cannot understand how the thought of those minds should have any more significance than the sound of the wind in the trees." (*Is Theology Poetry?*, the Oxford Socratic Club, 1944.)

The direction and conclusion of Lewis's argument is obvious. If the only alternative to "sheer self-contradictory idiocy" is "some tenacious belief in our power of reasoning," our minds and our thoughts clearly cannot be the product of blind chance and therefore solely of Nature, but must in some sense be dependent on, or illuminated by, some self-existent Reason outside the natural order: "Man is on the border line between the Natural and the Supernatural. Material events cannot produce spiritual activity, but the latter can be responsible for many of our actions on Nature. Will and Reason cannot depend on anything but themselves, but Nature can depend on Will and Reason, or, in other words, God created Nature." (*Bulverism or, The Foundation of Twentieth-century Thought,* Oxford Socratic Club, 1944).

It is only fair to say, at this point, that Lewis's assertion of the self-contradictory character of naturalism (defined as the atheistic doctrine that Nature is a closed, interlocked system) has not gone unchallenged.

In a paper read in 1947 to the Oxford Socratic Club, the philosopher, Elizabeth Anscombe, criticised Lewis for confusing the logical relationship between the premises and conclusions of propositions with the physical (and psychological) relation of cause and effect. By that she meant that it is always possible to examine an argument in order to see whether it obeys the laws of logic, and is therefore valid, whatever may be the causes, physical or psychological, which have led a particular person to accept its conclusions. In other words, according to Anscombe, the fact that our thinking involves a series of physical events in the brain does not in itself invalidate our chains of reasoning, or undermine the possibility of using our minds to obtain real knowledge.

Anscombe's assertion that the process of logical argument is not invalidated by the fact that it is also the result of physical events in the brain, however, fails to answer one obvious and critical question: how do we *know* that the laws of logic, and our conviction that a particular chain of reasoning is 'correct', are 'true' — and therefore a reflection of reality? Are they not *also* the end product of non-rational physical and psychological processes?

To illustrate this point, consider the following example. A person tells us that because some human beings are mad, and all the people in this room are human beings, *all* of them are mad. We reply, "your conclusion is false because your reasoning is incorrect, since it depends on the unstated and illogical assumption that if *some* human beings are mad, *all* human beings are mad — which is clearly absurd and contradictory since the very meaning of the term, 'some', in the phrase, 'some human beings are mad', implies by definition that there are *other* human beings who are *not* mad', in which case you have no logical grounds for saying that all the people in this room are mad". "Is that so?" the person replies. "Is my argument illogical? I confess it sometimes seems so to me, but since all our beliefs and conclusions are the end result of non-rational physical and psychological causes, I suspect our belief in the laws of logic is simply caused by something in our genetic inheritance, and a mutation has obviously occurred in my own genes as a consequence of which I am always convinced of the truth of illogical arguments."

Anscombe's error, in other words, as Dr Mascall pointed out in *Christian Theology And Natural Science*, is that her critique of Lewis' position only seems a good one "so long as we exclude from the sphere of application of the naturalistic theory the examiner's conviction of the validity of his examination [of a particular argument]." In fact, the whole debate about the self-contradictory character of naturalism (and therefore of atheism) echoes the old controversy surrounding determinism (the idea that 'free will' is an illusion).

Determinists who maintain that we have no free will undermine the credibility of their case, because if what they are saying is true, their own belief that we have no free will is *also* 'determined'. But if, for that reason, it is *inevitable*, how do we know it is true, since it is only the end product of inexorable, non-rational physical and psychological processes? For all these reasons, Dr Mascall was right to conclude: "...radical determinism about our mental processes is self-stultifying... If it is consistent, it must be applied not only to our volitions and our attitudes, but to our reasoning processes as well. Such plausibility as it has is due, I would maintain, to the fact that when it is asserted, an escape-clause is either explicitly included or, more often, implicitly assumed. It is held to apply to volitions and attitudes, but not to ratiocination; or, if it does apply to ratiocination in general, it does not apply to the ratiocination which its propounder makes use of in arguing for its truth."

Perhaps the clearest way of illustrating Lewis's argument about the relationship between Reason and matter, God and Nature, is to refer to his analogy of the wireless set (or radio). We listen to the news because although it comes to us through an inanimate, non-rational piece of machinery, we know that it *originates* with a real newsreader in a real studio, giving real information about the world we live in culled from eyewitness accounts by reporters in foreign cities. Similarly, although we think with our brains, our knowledge is not solely conditioned by them but is in some sense 'fed' from outside ourselves and the natural order by a self-existent Mind, or Divine power, behind or beyond the Universe. Hence Lewis's conclusion, in his 1944 Oxford Socratic Club paper, *Is Theology Poetry?*:

Granted that Reason is prior to matter and that the light of that primal Reason illuminates finite minds, I can understand how men should come, by observation and inference, to know a lot about the universe they live in. If, on the other hand, I swallow the scientific cosmology as a whole [meaning here, the atheistic naturalism popularised by H. G. Wells and Bertrand Russell], then not only can I not fit in Christianity, but I cannot even fit in science [because reasoning is discredited]... And this is to me the final test. This is how I distinguish dreaming and waking. When I am awake I can, in some degree, account for and study my dream. The dragon that pursued me last night can be fitted into my waking world. I know that there are such things as dreams: I know that I had eaten an indigestible dinner: I know that a man of my reading might be expected to dream of dragons. But while in the nightmare I could not have fitted in my waking experience. The waking world is judged more real because it can thus contain the dreaming world: the dreaming world is judged less real because it cannot contain the waking one. For the same reason I am certain that in passing from the scientific point of view to the theological, I have passed from dream to waking. Christian theology can fit in science, art, morality, and the sub-Christian religions. The scientific point of view cannot fit in any of these things, not even science itself. I believe in Christianity as I believe that the sun has risen not only because I see it but because by it I see everything else.

The theme of 'contingency' (i.e. lack of self-sufficiency) contrasted with 'self-existence', of the dependence of the natural on the supernatural, which — as Lewis showed — applies to the moral and epistemological realms (to our thinking and values), also — in his view — applied to the whole question of the actual existence of the Universe and of scientific laws.

Although he did not, in his writings, put much emphasis on the traditional cosmological argument for the existence of God (somewhat misleadingly called the 'First Cause' argument, and developed originally by Aristotle and Aquinas), Lewis did insist that the Universe is not self-explanatory, and that science cannot explain *why* it exists:

...why anything comes to be there at all, and whether there is anything behind the things science observes — something of a different kind — this is not a scientific question... Supposing science ever became complete so that it knew every single thing in the whole universe. Is it not plain that the questions, 'Why is there a universe?' 'Why does it go on as it does?' 'Has it any meaning?' would remain just as they were?" *(Mere Christianity*, p.31.)

Here we come up against what is perhaps the oldest and most persistent dispute between atheists and theists. To the former, the existence of the Universe — with all its creatures, structures and processes, from stars to starfish — is not a puzzle. It is simply 'there', a central and unalterable 'fact' whose workings we can and should investigate, but whose sheer presence and reality we must simply accept. Theists, on the other hand, regard this attitude as flying in the face of common sense and our actual experience of life. To them, the question why anything exists at all is a meaningful one because something cannot come from nothing, and therefore if something exists, it must either be the product or result of something else, or it must be self-existent. To deny this truth is the equivalent of saying that nothing *can*, after all, produce something — which is obviously absurd. Hence, when theists look at Nature, the first question they ask is: 'Does our knowledge of the Universe suggest that it is self-existent?' The answer, to them, is obviously 'no', since all organic life has a beginning and an end (animals and humans are born, live, and die), and inorganic structures and processes are subject to constant alteration and change. Even if the cosmos had no beginning and did not come into existence through some 'Big Bang' explosion (as many scientists believe), but instead is the product of the continuous creation or 'appearance' of matter, it still lacks that attribute of self-sufficiency which is the essence of self-existence, since the question that still arises is '*what* accounts for the creation or appearance of matter?' *Where*, so to speak, does the 'stuff' of the Universe continually come from? *Why* does change occur at all? *Who* or *what* brings it about?

The next step in the cosmological argument for the existence of God simply spells out the logical implication of this insight that the Universe is not self-sufficient but 'contingent'. Since it exists and is not self-caused, it must be the creation of some self-existent Power or Being 'beyond' or 'behind' Nature. As Lewis explained in a 1945 article discussing the relationship between prayer and scientific laws: "... the laws of Nature explain everything except the source of events. But this is rather a formidable exception. The laws, in one sense, cover the whole of reality except — well, except that continuous cataract of real events which makes up the actual universe. They explain everything except what we should ordinarily call 'everything'. The only thing they omit is — the whole universe..." ('The Laws of Nature', *Undeceptions:Essays on Theology and Ethics, p.54.*)

Atheist philosophers like the late Bertrand Russell, of course, do not accept this line of argument because they reject the notion that the Universe is 'contingent', as Russell made clear in 1948, when he debated the question of God's existence with the Catholic philosopher, F. J. Copleston, on BBC radio. But this attitude is hard to understand

and seems to evade rather than refute the cosmological argument. The other common objection to it, which Russell deployed in his famous polemic, *Why I Am Not A Christian*, is the utterly unconvincing one that if we insist that everything (including the Universe) must have a cause, then God must also have a cause (and our causal argument gets nowhere); or else, if God can be thought to be self-existent, then so can the Universe. But this misses the point. Russell, and atheists who think like him, misinterpret the cosmological argument because they will not acknowledge the crucial distinction that argument draws between *self-sufficient* and *dependent* being, treating them both, instead, as if they were the same kind of thing The cosmological argument does *not* say: 'everything must have a cause, therefore the Universe has a cause'; but: 'for contingent (dependent) being to exist, 'necessary' (self-existent) being must exist, but contingent being (the Universe) *does* exist, *therefore* necessary being (God) exists'. Or to put it all in Lewis's much more vivid and intelligible metaphorical language: "An egg which came from no bird is no more 'natural' than a bird which has existed from all eternity. And since the egg-bird sequence leads us to no plausible beginning, is it not reasonable to look for the real origin somewhere outside the sequence altogether? You have to go outside the sequence of engines, into the world of men, to find the real originator of the Rocket. Is it not equally reasonable to look outside Nature for the real Originator of the natural order?" ('Two Lectures', *Undeceptions*: *Essays on Theology and Ethics pp. 169-170.*)

A frequent objection to this position, which Russell, referring to the 'Heisenberg Uncertainty Principle', stated in his 1948 debate against F. J. Copleston, is that if physicists can conceive of sub-atomic events not having a cause, philosophers should acknowledge that the Universe does not need a cause. But this objection is really a red herring because no physical investigation can establish the absence of a cause, but only that in a particular case it was impossible to identify the causal *agent* behind some particular process. To believe otherwise is like saying that no-one wrote Shakespeare's plays because no-one alive today saw him (or anyone else) write them.

Despite the appeal of the cosmological argument (as deployed by Lewis and other philosophers down the centuries) to the common sense of the 'ordinary man', most contemporary professional philosophers deny its cogency and truthfulness, and the conventional view purveyed in most universities is that none of the traditional philosophical arguments for the existence of God (including the moral one and the 'argument from design') stand up to examination. Indeed, at least one strand of modern philosophy — starting with logical positivism — evades the whole issue of God's existence by asserting the meaninglessness of metaphysical speculation, the concept of God, and the terms used to describe Him. Readers or potential readers of C. S. Lewis, however, should not feel intimidated by the hostile climate of so much modern philosophy, or by the fact that philosophical theists are in a minority in most universities. They should remember instead that conventional wisdom in philosophy, as in other fields (economics being a good example), is frequently misguided and the product of prejudice and fashion as well as of rigorous logical analysis. Anyone who imagines that the philosophical arguments for the existence of God have been definitively demolished, should read the works of a whole army of 20th century philosophical theists. These include A.E. Taylor, D. L. Hawkins, Martin D'Arcy, E. L. Mascall, F. J. Copleston, J. R. Lucas, Keith Ward, Terry Miethe, Basil Mitchell, and Richard Swinburne — and there are other names which could be mentioned. In these books and papers (some of which are mentioned in Appendix B at the end of this volume) the open-minded student will discover both robust and reasoned affirmations of the existence of God, and detailed critiques of the assumptions and arguments of the modern critics of theism — especially of those who maintain that religious and metaphysical concepts and language are meaningless.

Much of the scepticism and hostility towards theism, and the whole idea of a God outside Nature who created it, undoubtedly derived, in Lewis's opinion, from the popular scientific cosmology which dominates the modern mind, and which he termed 'evolutionism' — by which he meant the idea that gradual development from small beginnings is the essential process behind all phenomena, from the creation of the Universe to the formation of human consciousness and moral values. 'Evolutionism', however, which Lewis contrasted with the idea of evolution in the purely biological field, is an inadequate cosmological theory because, as we have seen, it cannot account for logical thought and moral awareness. In any case, argued Lewis, it is implausible on closer scrutiny:

The modern acquiescence in universal evolutionism is a kind of optical illusion, produced by attending exclusively to the owl's emergence from the egg. We are taught from childhood to notice how the perfect oak grows from the acorn and to forget that the acorn itself was dropped by a perfect oak. We are reminded constantly that the adult human being was an embryo, never that the life of the embryo came from two adult human beings. We love to notice that the express engine of today is the descendant of the 'Rocket'; we do not equally remember that the 'Rocket' springs not from some even more rudimentary engine, but from something much more perfect and complicated than itself —namely, a man of genius. The obviousness or naturalness which most people seem to find in the idea of emergent evolution thus seems to be a pure hallucination. (*Is Theology Poetry?* 1944, Oxford Socratic Club Paper)

The real reason, argued Lewis, for the popularity of this flawed atheistic cosmology is that it has all the qualities of a myth, one moreover with a strong poetic appeal to the imagination.

Echoing the fairy tale themes of the younger son and the ugly duckling, evolutionism portrays the accidental emergence of life and intelligence in the Universe as a heroic struggle against the odds whose tragic grandeur is ensured by the fact that it is doomed to ultimate defeat. The whole Universe will eventually run down and every form of life will be banished from every inch of infinite space. "Such a world drama," Lewis rightly concludes, "appeals to every part of us". (*Is Theology Poetry?*)

The prestige of modern science, and the popularity of the 'evolutionist' cosmology it has spawned, has not only helped to turn people's minds away from orthodox Christianity, theism, and metaphysical speculation, but — wrote Lewis — has also produced a reductionist mentality which cannot see the wood for the trees when examining human consciousness and its offshoots — love, moral awareness, and religious experience. As a result, it fails to attach proper weight to the evidence for the existence of God from religious experience, and we thus have the irony that the very atheists and sceptics who tell us not to believe anything except on the basis of empirical evidence, ignore or discount the significant evidential fact that millions of people today and down the ages can testify to the reality of God from their own experience of prayer, meditation, and corporate worship, as well as through occasional special encounters in the form of miracles and visions.

As Lewis puts it, there is a difference between 'looking at' something and 'looking along' it. If, for instance, you are standing in a dark toolshed looking *at* a beam of light coming through a crack in the door, you see the beam, and the specks of dust floating in it, and everything else is in darkness. If you then move so that the beam falls on your eyes, and you are therefore looking *along* it, you see something different: no longer the beam itself, but a glimpse of green leaves moving on the branches of a tree outside the shed and beyond that, the sun. Looking along the beam, and looking at it, are very different experiences.

> But this is only a very simple example of the difference between looking at and looking along. A young man meets a girl. The whole world looks different when he sees her. Her voice reminds him of something he has been trying to remember all his life, and ten minutes casual chat with her is more precious than all the favours that all other women in the world could grant. He is, as they say, 'in love'. Now comes a scientist and describes this young man's experience from the outside. For him it is all an affair of the young man's genes and a recognised biological stimulus. That is the difference between looking *along* the sexual impulse and looking *at* it...
>
> As soon as you have grasped this simple distinction, it raises a question. You get one experience of a thing when you look along it and another when you look at it. Which is the 'true' or 'valid' experience? Which tells you most about the thing? And you can hardly ask that question without noticing that for the last fifty years or so everyone has been taking the answer for granted. It has been assumed without discussion that if you want the true account of religion you must go, not to religious people, but to anthropologists; that if you want the true account of sexual love you must go, not to lovers, but to psychologists; that if you want to understand some 'ideology' (such as medieval chivalry or the nineteenth-century idea of a ' gentleman'), you must listen not to those who lived inside it, but to sociologists."
> (Meditation In A Toolshed', *Undeceptions: Essays in Theology and Ethics, pp.171-2.*)

All this does not mean, as Lewis recognised, that the 'inside' view of a love affair or a religion is always or necessarily correct or true. We can be deceived by our emotions, by other people, and by our experiences, but to discount — for that reason — *all* 'inside' experiences is untenable:

> You discount them in order to think more accurately. But you can't think at all — and therefore, of course, can't think accurately — if you have nothing to think *about*. A physiologist, for example, can study pain and find out that it 'is' (whatever *is* means) such and such neural events. But the word *pain* would have no meaning for him unless he had 'been inside' by actually suffering. If he had never looked *along* pain he simply wouldn't know what he was looking *at*. ('Meditation In A Toolshed', *Undeceptions: Essays in Theology and Ethics*, p. 173.)

It is still, of course, true that owing to the possibility of self-deception, internal evidence from religious experience cannot be used to prove the existence of God to someone who has never had such an experience, but the fact that large numbers of people of all nations, types, and temperaments appear to have had some internal experience of God, should be regarded by an open-minded person as some evidence (albeit inconclusive) for the truth of theism. In addition, Lewis argued, atheists and sceptics cannot ignore the perhaps more objectively significant fact that religious consciousness exists at all. Yet is this not puzzling? How can human beings, if their minds are merely the end product of the accidental collision of atoms, even *conceive* of the possibility that there might be something behind or beyond the Universe? If we are simply parts of a closed, mechanistic system, why do so many of us imagine that there is a reality outside ourselves and the world we live in, to which we are somehow connected? And why does this religious awareness show no signs of dying away with the progress of knowledge, and affect scientists and philosophers as much as artists and poets, engineers and astronomers as well as children and housewives? We are so used to the existence of the religious impulse, in others even if not in ourselves, that we fail to perceive the strangeness of its presence and persistence in the human psyche if, as atheists believe, there really is no God and therefore no obvious source of religious consciousness.

> How could an idiotic universe have produced creatures whose mere dreams are so much stronger, better, subtler than itself?... Do fish complain of the sea for being wet? Or if they did, would that fact itself

not strongly suggest that they had not always been, or would not always be, purely aquatic creatures? If you are really a product of a materialistic universe, how is it that you don't feel at home there? ('Encounter with Light', *A Mind Awake*, p. 22.)

How, in addition, do we account for the existence of what Lewis termed the 'inconsolable longing' — that yearning in so many for that Something outside themselves and their actual experience of this world, which cannot be identified with any concrete experience of beauty or love, though it often communicates itself *through* them? It cannot simply be dismissed as wishful thinking because this begs the question of *why*, if atheism is correct, the products of a mechanistic Universe *want* something outside it?

> ... though I do not believe (I wish I did) that my desire for Paradise proves that I shall enjoy it, I think it a pretty good indication that such a thing exists and that some men will. A man may love a woman and not win her; but it would be very odd if the phenomenon called 'falling in love' occurred in a sexless world." (*Transposition and Other Addresses*, ch. 2)

Man's religious impulse includes another significant oddity, said Lewis, equally difficult to account for on atheistic assumptions: namely, consciousness of the 'Numinous' — that sense of fear akin to awe people feel in the presence of the supernatural, as when they see (or think they see) a ghost, and which is not derived from that immediate consciousness of danger to themselves that they would feel if a tiger came into the room.:

> We must insist that dread and awe are in a different dimension from fear. They are in the nature of an interpretation Man gives to the universe, or an impression he gets from it; and just as no enumeration of the physical qualities of a beautiful object could ever include its beauty, or give the faintest hint of what we mean by beauty to a creature without aesthetic experience, so no factual description of any human environment could include the uncanny and the Numinous or even hint at them. (*The Problem of Pain*, p. 16.)

Despite the many powerful objections to atheism and its materialistic picture of reality and the Universe, one apparent escape route remains for those convinced of the untenability of materialism but unwilling to embrace the concept of the living, active, creative God of Christian theology. That escape route is into pantheism, the view that God and the Universe are one, and which in modern times usually takes the form of belief in a creative evolutionary Life Force which has given rise to consciousness as well as producing snow flakes and galaxies. According to this philosophy, sometimes described as 'emergent evolutionism', everything that exists is a manifestation of this Life Force, which has been evolving and developing for millions of years, and is continuing its upward ascent.

This pantheistic outlook is extremely popular and widespread because it appears to satisfy the religious impulse of modern man while at the same time remaining in tune with today's dominant 'scientific' cosmology. It was reflected in the popular evolutionist philosophy of the unorthodox Catholic thinker, Teilhard De Chardin, and has exerted a powerful influence on popular culture through films like Walt Disney's *Fantasia* and Stephen Spielberg's *Star Wars*, and its sequels. Unfortunately, however, as C. S. Lewis pointed out, pantheistic naturalism suffers from two fatal flaws.

First of all, it wholly fails to explain the existence of our moral consciousness — our awareness of moral values and moral obligation — because its assertion that 'God' (or the Life Force) and the Universe are one, abolishes the distinction between good and evil since everything that happens and exists is simply a different manifestation of the same underlying Universal Spirit. Secondly, and equally fatally, it cannot account — any more than strict materialism — for the existence of our minds and our capacity to reason:

> It is, of course, possible to suppose that when all the atoms of the universe got into a certain relation... they would give rise to a universal consciousness. And it might have thoughts. And it might cause those thoughts to pass through our minds. But unfortunately its own thoughts, on this supposition, would be the product of non-rational causes and therefore, by the rule which we use daily, they would have no validity. This cosmic mind would be, just as much as our own minds, the product of mindless Nature. We have not escaped from the difficulty, we have only put it a stage further back. The cosmic mind

will help us only if we put it at the beginning, if we suppose it to be, not the product of the total system, but the basic, original, self-existent Fact which exists in its own right. But to admit *that* sort of cosmic mind is to admit a God outside Nature, a transcendent and supernatural God. This route, which looked like offering an escape, really leads us round again to the place we started from. There is, then, a God who is not a part of Nature." (*Miracles*, pp. 34-5.)

It is with such arguments that Lewis reminds us of a truth expressed by Bacon, as long ago as the sixteenth century: "A little philosophy inclineth man's mind to atheism, but depth in philosophy bringeth men's minds about to religion." (*Essays* 16, Atheism.)

3. In Defence of Christianity

Having surveyed in the previous chapter C.S. Lewis's reasons for rejecting atheism, we find ourselves facing the two great questions which most of his theological writings addressed and attempted to answer. If God exists and created Nature and mankind, and there is thus an Absolute Goodness behind the Universe, what explains the existence of evil and suffering? Why, moreover, should we believe Christianity's claim that it alone, of all religions, not only gives the truest answer to this terrible question but also contains the fullest revelation of the nature of God and of His purposes for mankind?

Before considering Lewis's answers to these questions, it must at once be emphasised that he did not become a Christian or advocate Christianity because he thought it was good for society or benefited humanity, or because it comforts, strengthens or improves individuals. Lewis believed in it and defended its claims because he became convinced that Christianity is *true* — that it, and it alone, presents an accurate picture of reality.

> ... Christianity is not a patent medicine. Christianity claims to give an accounts of *facts* — to tell you what the real universe is like. Its account of the universe may be true, or it may not, and once the question is really before you, then your natural inquisitiveness must make you want to know the answer. If Christianity is untrue, then no honest man will want to believe it, however helpful it might be: if it is true, every honest man will want to believe it, even if it gives him no help at all. (*Undeceptions: Essays on Theology and Ethics*, 'Man or Rabbit?', pp. 81-2.)

What, then, returning to our main theme, *does* Christianity affirm about

God, evil and the human condition, and why should we believe it?

Its first great affirmation is that God is Love. This apparently banal and conventional statement is not only a necessary implication of the truth that God is the source of our moral consciousness and therefore Good; but, Lewis pointed out, is also vital to our understanding of both the Christian doctrine of the Trinity and the purpose behind creation, the two being closely interlinked. As Lewis put it, love is a relation between persons. But if this is true, the phrase 'God is Love' has no meaning unless God contains or consists of at least two Persons, because if He were only a single Person, then before the world was made He was not Love. What Christians therefore mean by the statement 'God is Love' is that: "the living dynamic activity of love has been going on in God forever and has created everything else". And that "living, dynamic activity of love has been going on in God" between what Christian theology describes as the three Persons of the Trinity: the Father, the Son, and the Holy Spirit.

At this point two objections immediately spring to mind. The first is conceptual: how can God be a unity of three Persons? How can three Persons be One? Secondly, on what grounds and by what authority do Christians presume to know the Trinitarian nature of God, when this conception of God is unique to themselves and not shared by any other world religion?

A full answer to the second question will emerge when we look at the whole subject of the Incarnation and the status and claims of Christ, as Lewis understood it, but the conceptual objection can be met head-on straightaway. If careful reasoning and internal experience leads us to acknowledge the reality of God — that is, of a Being who is self-exist-ent, the Creator of the Universe, and the Power behind that Moral Law we find written on our hearts and consciences, we also ought to ac-knowledge the obvious truth that our understanding of God is bound to be partial and incomplete. The difference between Einstein and an amoeba is as nothing compared to the ontological gulf between us (as dependent creatures) and our eternal, self-existent Creator. Consequently we should not be surprised by the inability of our minds to fully grasp the nature of God or the consciousness of the Godhead. What counts in weighing the truth of any particular statement about God's nature and attributes is the *degree* to which it is comprehensible to our minds and transparent to the intellect. Even if we can only 'look through a glass darkly' at the idea of "God in Three Persons, Blessed Trinity" (to quote the words of a well known hymn), can we — by the use of analogies — see or grasp *enough* of its meaning to be confident that it conveys a true insight about God, one which may go *beyond* our reason but not *against* it?

C.S. Lewis insisted we could, pointing out that whereas many people

feel that the mysterious something which is behind all other things must be more than a person... Christians are the only people who offer any idea of what a being that is beyond personality could be like. All the other people, though they say that God is beyond personality, really think of Him as something impersonal: that is, as something less than personal. If you are looking for something super-personal, something more than a person, then it is not a question of choosing between the Christian idea and the other ideas. The Christian idea is the only one on the market. (*Mere Christianity,* p.136)

The analogy Lewis used to explain the Trinity was that of the cube:

On the human level one person is one being, and any two persons are two separate beings — just as, in two dimensions (say on a flat sheet of paper) one square is one-figure, and any two squares are two separate figures. On the Divine level you still find personalities; but up there you find them combined in new ways which we, who do not live on that level, cannot imagine. In God's dimension, so to speak, you find a being who is three Persons while remaining one Being, just as a cube is six squares while remaining one cube. Of course we cannot fully conceive a Being like that: just as, if we were so made that we perceived only two dimensions in space we could never properly imagine a cube. But we can get a sort of faint notion of it. (*Mere Christianity,* pp. 138-9)

Thus we see that the Trinitarian conception of God is not some fantastic piece of theological gobbledegook dreamed up by the early Church, but a perfectly rational formulation about the Divine nature based on revelation (mainly but not solely through and in relation to Christ) but also appealing to reason, since it shows how God can be self-existent Love and therefore the source of human love. The concept of the Trinity also

helps to answer a real and difficult question about the relationship between God and goodness: is what is good simply what God commands
or does God only command what is good?

If good is to be *defined* as what God commands, then the goodness
of God Himself is emptied of meaning and the commands of an omnipotent evil spirit would have the same claim on us as those of a righteous
God. If on the other hand, God only commands what is good, we seem
to be admitting a cosmic diarchy, or even making God Himself the mere
executor of a law somehow external and antecedent to His own being.

Having raised the problem, however, Lewis finds the solution in the
reminder that the limitations of our creaturely perceptions cannot help
sometimes but distort our perspective of God, and cause us, if we are
not careful to take our ignorance seriously, to pose what are in reality
nonsense questions. Hence, again, the importance of grasping the truth
that although God is personal, He is *more* than a Person:

> God is not merely good, but goodness; goodness is not merely divine,
> but God.
>
> These may seem fine-spun speculations: yet I believe that nothing
> short of this can save us. A Christianity which does not see moral and
> religious experience converging to meet at infinity, not at a negative
> infinity, but in the positive infinity of the living yet superpersonal
> God, has nothing, in the long run, to divide it from devil worship; and
> a philosophy which does not accept value as eternal and objective can
> lead us only to ruin. ('The Poison of Subjectivism', *Christian Reflec-
> tions*, pp. 80-81.)

Atheists may still object that for all Lewis's ingenuity and eloquence, he
fails — in their eyes — to resolve the conceptual difficulty about the
relationship between theism and ethics, but they in turn face a much
more serious problem. They not only have to explain why it is unreasonable for theists to assert the self-evident truth that if God exists and
created us, we can hardly expect to be able to understand *everything*
about Him: they must also face the fact, discussed in the preceding
chapter, that on *their* assumptions they can neither account for our moral
consciousness and provide an objective basis for morality, *nor* can they
explain how the human mind can know anything or reason. If, therefore, the only choice we face is between a partial explanation of moral

and metaphysical reality which makes some sort of sense, and an atheistic philosophy which makes no sense at all, it is surely reasonable to
consider the claims of Christianity seriously, and keep an open mind
about such unexpected but still comprehensible doctrines as the Trinity.
As Lewis summed the matter up:

> There is no good complaining that these statements are difficult. Chris-
> tianity claims to be telling us about another world, about something
> behind the world we can touch and hear and see. You may think the
> claim false; but if it were true, what it tells us would be bound to be
> difficult — at least as difficult as modern Physics, and for the same
> reason... If Christianity was something we were making up, of course
> we could make it easier. But it is not. We cannot compete, in simplic-
> ity, with people who are inventing religions. How could we? We are
> dealing with Fact. Of course anyone can be simple if he has no facts
> to bother about. (*Mere Christianity,* p.134)

Having taken a brief but necessary first glance at Lewis's interpretation
of the nature and relevance of the Christian doctrine of the Trinity, we
come to the second great truth proclaimed by Christianity and revealed
in the opening pages of the Bible: "In the beginning", to quote the *Book
of Genesis,* "God created the heavens and the earth", all living creatures
— including Man, and declared, at the end of it all, that everything He
had made "was *very good*". Thus God's revelation of Himself through
the Bible, (and the notion of Divine revelation through Scripture will be
discussed later), both confirms the conclusions of rational philosophical
speculation: that God exists; that He is Good; that He created the Universe and is separate from it; *and*, in addition, emphasises the stark and
startling fact that there was *nothing* evil in the beginning. Goodness, in
short, is original, whereas evil must — in some sense — be secondary
and derivative.

The plausibility of this revelation — its agreement with common
sense and reason — becomes obvious, argued Lewis, as soon as you
compare it with the only possible alternative explanation for the existence of evil: which is dualism — the doctrine that Good and Evil are
two equal and opposite powers eternally waging war against each other
for the mastery of the Universe.

While dualism has the merit of regarding good and evil as objective moral categories, and therefore does not deny or belittle the reality of our moral consciousness, ít is an untenable and unsatisfactory philosophy because it cannot explain how, on its own premises, we can *know* that the Good Power is good, and the Evil one, evil. Since you can only compare two things by measuring them against a common standard, dualism either implies that our reason for saying one power is good and the other, evil, is subjective — merely an expression of arbitrary personal preference; or it implies the existence of some third thing in addition to the two powers: some law, for instance, or rule of good, to which one of the powers conforms while the other does not. But to admit that makes nonsense of dualism, since it implies that there is, after all, another *higher* standard or power which is the *real* Ultimate Goodness or God. The truth is therefore inescapable: goodness must be original and supreme if our awareness of moral obligation and the existence of the Moral Law are not to be dismissed as illusions.

> The same point can be made in a different way. If Dualism is true, then the bad Power must be a being who likes badness for its own sake. But in reality we have no experience of anyone liking badness just because it is bad. The nearest we can get to it is in cruelty. But in real life people are cruel for one or two reasons — either because they are sadists, that is, because they have a sexual perversion which makes cruelty a cause of sensual pleasure to them, or else for the sake of something they are going to get out of it — money, or power, or safety. But pleasure, money, power, and safety are all, as far as they go, good things. The badness consists in pursuing them by the wrong method, or in the wrong way, or too much... Goodness is, so to speak, itself: badness is only spoiled goodness. And there must be something good first before it can be spoiled. (*Mere Christianity,* pp. 45-6.)

In other words, the Bad Power has to exist and possess intelligence and will in order to do evil, but since existence, intelligence and will are good in themselves, it follows that its capacity to do evil is derived from the Good Power.

The conclusion to which this reasoning leads is the one revealed in Christian theology and spelt out in the opening chapters of *Genesis* (and elsewhere in the Bible): evil and suffering came into the Universe (as they could only have done) following a rebellion against God by created beings to whom God had given free will, and with it, the terrible opportunity of rejecting Him and setting their wills against His.

> Some people think that they can imagine a creature which was free but had no possibility of going wrong; I cannot. If a thing is free to be good it is also free to be bad. And free will is what has made evil possible. Why, then, did God give them free will? Because free will, though it makes evil possible, is also the only thing that makes possible any love or goodness or joy worth having. A world of automata —of creatures that worked like machines — would hardly be worth creating. The happiness which God designs for His higher creatures is the happiness of being freely, voluntarily united to Him and to each other in an ecstasy of love and delight compared with which the most rapturous love between a man and a woman on this earth is mere milk and water. And for that they must be free. (*Mere Christianity* pp. 48-9.)

Although we can perceive, by our own unaided reason, that evil must have originated in the remote past in some such act of creaturely rebellion, and that it could only have been made possible by the wonderful but terrible gift of free will, it is obvious that we could not know the true details of that dreadful event unless it had been directly revealed to the human race by God. Christians, of course, Lewis among them, believe that this is precisely what He has done through the Bible. But before looking more closely at the Biblical story of the Fall, and Lewis's interpretation of it, it is appropriate to make one obvious preliminary observation about the whole subject of 'special revelation'.

If God exists and created Man in His own image, it is surely reasonable to suppose that He wishes to communicate with the human beings He loves, especially if — through the sins of our remote ancestors — the whole human race has gone astray and is therefore in desperate need of God's help and guidance. Consequently no one with an open mind should be shocked by the idea that God may speak to individuals through visions, prayer, meditation, or in other ways; nor should anyone be startled by the notion that God may have spoken to the human race through specially chosen messengers down the centuries, and that these 'messages from Heaven' have been collected together to form sacred books, or scriptures. Whilst the test of the authenticity of revelation is not a matter which can be properly discussed in this book (readers interested in the whole question of the reliability of the Bible should consult Appendix B), this much can be said here, and is relevant to our consideration of C.S. Lewis's writings: the internal coherence in terms of reason and logic of a particular Biblical doctrine or story, is evidence in favour of its truthfulness, especially if it accords with personal and historical experience. By *that* standard, the Biblical explanation of the origin of evil, and its story of the Fall of Man, has — as Lewis demonstrated — the 'ring of truth', as we shall see in a moment.

Turning back, then, to this subject, we note that the Bible attributes the first great act of rebellion against God by the human race to a process of temptation initiated by a mighty evil spirit described throughout Scripture as the Serpent, Satan, or the Devil — a created spirit being who was originally the mightiest and most beautiful of all archangels, and who once stood — according to the Bible — in the immediate presence of God, and was originally good. As a result, Christians believe that the Fall of Man was preceded by an earlier 'Fall' in the purely spiritual, angelic realm, and since both this event and the origin of Satan are vividly and poignantly portrayed in Scripture, as poetically as in Milton's *Paradise Lost*, it is worth quoting some relevant Biblical passages before considering Lewis's views on these matters and the credibility of his explanations.

The Book of *Ezekiel*, chapter 28: 12-17, vividly describes Satan's original character and status, as these extracts make clear:

> You were the signet of perfection,
> full of wisdom
> and perfect in beauty.
> You were in Eden, the garden of God;
> ...
> you were on the holy mountain of God;
> in the midst of the stones of fire you walked.
> You were blameless in your ways
> from the day you were created,
> till iniquity was found in you
> ...

And what was that "iniquity" which inspired Satan's rebellion against God? Pride. To return to *Ezekiel* 28: 17:

Your heart was proud because of your beauty;
you corrupted your wisdom for the sake of your splendour
...

The Book of *Isaiah*, Chapter 14: 12-15, is even more explicit in its description of Satan's rebellion and fall from Heaven:

How you are fallen from heaven,
O Day Star, son of Dawn!
How you are cut down to the ground,
you who laid the nations low!
You said in your heart,
I will ascend to heaven;
above the stars of God
I will set my throne on high

...
I will ascend above the heights of the clouds,
I will make myself like the Most High ...

What is valuable and relevant about these passages is what they reveal about the origin of sin and the relationship between Pride and rebelliousness against God; but the reasons *why* Pride is a sin and the origin of all evil will become clearer when we come to deal with Lewis's interpretation of the Biblical account of the Fall of Man. In the meantime we must note that according to the Bible, the Devil is not a figment of the imagination, a spooky mythical figure haunting legends and stories, but a real person — a supernatural power who is the focus and source of evil, and the Enemy of God and Man.

Now, of course, as Lewis well knew, this statement seems so outlandish to the modern secularised Western mind, that it is commonly dismissed as a ridiculous superstition, but to treat the matter in this light is itself irrational. Do those who are shocked by all talk of the Devil react like that because they have really taken the trouble to think the matter through and have concluded that it is a lot of nonsense, or are their reactions simply an unreflecting emotional reflex conditioned by the cultural climate of the modern scientific age? Is it really so hard to believe in the existence of Satan when we see how much evil there is in the world and how often the worst get to the top? And what about the whole area of the occult? Is the centuries-old practice of witchcraft and 'black magic' simply a manifestation of human superstition or insanity, or does it possibly offer some circumstantial evidence for the existence of Satan? Bertrand Russell once suggested, only half in jest, that the world was made by the Devil while God wasn't looking. After a century which has witnessed the monstrous crimes of men like Pol Pot and Hitler, one is tempted to agree with him.

However, despite the initial plausibility of Russell's bitterly humorous speculations, Christian theology — informed by Biblical revelation — teaches that everything in creation was originally good but that goodness turned into evil in Satan through the corruption of his heart by Pride. The famous story in *Genesis* of the temptation and Fall of Man in the Garden of Eden describes how Satan subsequently taught this sin to the human race.

Since the double Fall of Satan and Man is, according to Christians, the origin of all evil and suffering, an adequate appreciation of what it entailed is essential if we are to understand how and why it separated the human race from God with literally mortal consequences in time and eternity. Only then is it possible to make any sense of the doctrine of the Incarnation — of the life and atoning death and resurrection of Christ, which is the heart of the Christian Gospel.

Here, Lewis's writings reveal a profound understanding of the nature and root of sin, an understanding derived from observation and introspection and most clearly expressed in *The Problem of Pain*, in his book on Milton — *A Preface to Paradise Lost*, and in *Mere Christianity*.

According to Lewis, the key to understanding the heinousness of Pride and the nature of the Fall lies in a correct appreciation of the doctrine (and fact) of Creation, and all that it implies for the proper relationship between God and His creatures — whether angelic or human.

If God is Love, the self-existent Creator of the Universe, and the Moral Law behind all things, it follows that He is not only the source of all life but also the fountain and origin of all beauty, truth and goodness. He is the source of our very ability to love, think, and create. This means that we cannot grasp ultimate reality without at the same time being forced to recognise our derivative, creaturely status of total dependence on God. We are also compelled to recognise that it is to His *love* that we owe our very being since He was never under any necessity to create us in the first place. As Lewis puts it:

> In God there is no hunger that needs to be filled, only plenteousness that desires to give... to be sovereign of the universe is no great matter to God. In Himself, at home in 'the land of the Trinity', he is Sovereign of a far greater realm. We must keep always before our eyes that vision of Lady Julian's in which God carried in His hand a little object like a nut, and that nut was 'all that is made'. God, who needs nothing, loves into existence wholly superfluous creatures in order that He may love and perfect them. (*The Four Loves*, ch. 6)

Two conclusions follow from this analysis, of which the first is a moral one.

Given who God is, and that we owe Him everything, He merits our love, worship and obedience. We owe Him our allegiance and our selves not only out of gratitude for the gift of life, but because it is the only sane and rational response to the supreme revelation of His love, majesty, beauty and goodness. To be unwilling to respond to God in this way is to be like a plant that refuses to grow towards the sunlight. Secondly, since God is the Creator, and therefore the fountain of all goodness and the source of all our mental and physical powers, it is irrational to resist His will or disobey His commands since He must, in the nature of things, both know and want what is best for us. To argue with God and to reject Him is therefore to challenge Omniscient Love and to cut ourselves off from the source of all life and truth.

Now what the Bible describes in its account of the double Fall of Satan and mankind, is precisely the poisoning and destruction of the formerly happy relationship between creatures and Creator.

"From the moment a creature becomes aware of God as God and of itself as self, the terrible alternative of choosing God or self for the centre is opened to it," wrote Lewis in *The Problem of Pain*, and that choosing of the "self for the centre" is what lies at the heart of the Fall. The harmony and joy that once prevailed in the Universe, according to the Bible, was first shattered in Heaven because Satan, turning in upon himself and away from God, resented and rejected his creaturely status and sought to usurp God's Lordship over Creation. As Lewis put it unforgettably in *A Preface to Paradise Lost*: "In the midst of a world of light and love, of song and feast and dance, he could find nothing to think of more interesting than his own prestige." But:

> a creature revolting against a creator is revolting against the source of his own powers — including even his power to revolt... It is like the scent of a flower trying to destroy the flower. As a consequence the same rebellion which means misery for the feelings and corruption for the will, means nonsense for the intellect.

Lewis's reference to Satan turning away from "A world of light and love, of song and feast and dance", underlines one of the most obvious but important truths about the evil consequences of Pride. Its monomaniac exaltation of the self at the expense of God and others leads to misery and self-destruction, because it not only narrows the focus of existence to an endless introspective obsession with one's own ego and status, but destroys the very possibility of love, knowledge, and true contentment.

> In coming to understand anything we are rejecting the facts as they are for us in favour of the facts as they are. The primary impulse of each is to maintain and aggrandise himself. The secondary impulse is to go out of the self, to correct its provincialism and heal its loneliness. In love, in virtue, in the pursuit of knowledge, and in the reception of the arts, we are doing this. Obviously this process can be described either as an enlargement or as a temporary annihilation of the self. But that is an old paradox; 'he that loseth his life shall save it.' (*An Experiment in Criticism*, Epilogue.)

Pride, on the other hand, argued Lewis in *Mere Christianity*, is *essentially* competitive. It gets no pleasure out of having something, only out of having more of it than someone else. We say that people are proud of their wealth, intelligence or good looks but they are not. They are only proud of being wealthier, or more intelligent and better-looking than others. It is the *comparison* that causes pride: the pleasure of being above the rest. Hence, concluded Lewis, Christians are right in their conviction that it is Pride which has been the chief cause of misery in every family and nation since the world began.

The interwoven themes of pride, self-centredness and rebellion, and their connection with suffering and death, come out with particular clarity in the famous account of the Fall of Man in *Genesis*, starting with the temptation of Eve and ending with the expulsion of Adam and Eve from the Garden of Eden (Paradise). The kernel of the story involves the breaking of God's commandment not to eat the fruit "of the tree of the knowledge of good and evil", and before considering Lewis's interpretation of this event and its consequences, it is helpful to remind ourselves of some of the relevant Biblical passages:

> Now the serpent was more subtle than any other wild creature that the Lord God had made. He said to the woman, 'Did God say, "You shall not eat of any tree of the garden?"' And the woman said to the serpent, 'We may eat of the fruit of the trees of the garden; but God said, "You shall not eat of the fruit of the tree which is in the midst of the garden, neither shall you touch it, lest you die."' But the serpent said to the woman, 'You will not die. God knows that when you eat of it your eyes will be opened, and you will be like God, knowing good and evil.' So when the woman saw that the tree was good for food, and that it was a delight to the eyes, and that the tree was to be desired to make one wise, she took of its fruit and ate; and she also gave some to her husband, and he ate. Then the eyes of both were opened, and they knew that they were naked; and they sewed fig leaves together and made themselves aprons. And they heard the sound of the Lord God walking in the garden in the cool of the day, and the man and his wife hid themselves from the presence of the Lord God among the trees of the garden. (*Genesis* 3:1-8.)

The story in *Genesis* then goes on to describe, in further detail, the tragic progression (now so familiar to us!) from disobedience to consciousness of guilt, from guilt to confession, and then from confession to judgement, of which the keynote is death: "In the sweat of your face you shall eat bread till you return to the ground, for out of it you were taken; you are dust, and to dust you shall return." (*Genesis* 3:19)

The central clue to understanding the Fall of Man lies in grasping the significance of God's commandment not to eat the fruit "of the knowledge of good and evil", and here we at once encounter a common and seemingly powerful objection to the whole theological conception of the Fall. The story in *Genesis*, it is argued, quite apart from the modern scientific objections to it (which will be examined in due course), is the product of a reactionary and obscurantist religious outlook whose conception of the good life is that of a Universe of ignorant and childish savages totally subservient to a tyrannical and Scrooge-like Deity. Such a theology, people protest, prefers unquestioning obedience to the search for knowledge and truth, and is rooted in fear and the abject worship of power. To quote the eloquent words of the late Bertrand Russell, whose whole outlook typifies the secular humanism of the twentieth century:

> The whole conception of God is a conception derived from the ancient Oriental despotisms. It is a conception quite unworthy of free men. When you hear people in church debasing themselves and saying that they are miserable sinners, and all the rest of it, it seems contemptible and not worthy of self-respecting human beings. We ought to stand up and look the world frankly in the face. A good world needs knowledge, kindliness, and courage; it does not need a regretful hankering after the past, or a fettering of the free intelligence by the words uttered long ago by ignorant men. It needs a fearless outlook and a free intelligence. (*Why I Am Not A Christian.*)

But whilst Russell's motivation and rhetoric are splendid, the defects in his argument and in the outlook he represents have already been clearly exposed in the preceding chapter on C.S. Lewis's reasons for rejecting atheism, and they have also been implicitly answered in the course of our current examination of the nature of God and the evil and irrationality of Pride. To summarise: only the existence of God can explain both the existence of the Universe, the possibility of knowledge, and our moral and religious consciousness. But if we know that God exists, and can see what are His necessary attributes and character, it is obviously absurd to imagine that we can be justified in attacking His motives or criticising His commands, as if we could know better than Omniscience. It is equally ridiculous to regard the whole business of worshipping God (that activity by which love naturally overflows into praise) as something unreasonable and beneath our dignity. As Lewis explains:

> We must not think Pride is something God forbids because He is offended at it, or that Humility is something He demands as due to His own dignity — as if God Himself was proud. He is not in the least worried

about His dignity. The point is, He wants you to know Him: wants to
give you Himself. And He and you are two things of such a kind that if
you really get into any kind of touch with Him you will, in fact, be humble — delightedly humble... (*Mere Christianity,* pp. 111-12.)

In other words, what Lewis is again emphasising, is the *irrationality* of
rejecting or disobeying our Creator. An atheist may honestly disbelieve
in the existence of God, but to dismiss the very *idea* of God as a tyrannical concept, shows a complete failure to understand (if only imagina-
tively) what the notion of God necessarily entails. After all, what response other than worship is appropriate in an encounter with Absolute
Goodness, Beauty and Love? Furthermore, the idea that God's prohibition against eating from the tree "of the knowledge of good and evil" is
repugnant because it reflects some arbitrary (and therefore unjustified)
act of the Divine Will, misses a very important point about the nature of
the choice facing unfallen Man and the consequences that must necessarily flow from disobedience to God.

Since Man was primarily created to know, love and enjoy God —
that is, to be united, of his own free will, with the source of all life,
beauty and goodness — that voluntary allegiance to God could only be
fully expressed by an act of unconditional obedience motivated by unconditional love. But what conceivable test of Man's love for God could
there be, in a perfect and unfallen world, except a choice between accepting or rejecting His will? And how could the occasion of such a
choice arise other than in the form of some prohibition the rationale of
which was beyond an unfallen creature's understanding? Only if the
reason for obeying a particular prohibition lay *solely* in a sense of obligation rooted in love, humility, and trust (the proper attitude of creature
to Creator) could that act of obedience be a true expression of unconditional allegiance. This point is given particularly vivid fictional
expression in Lewis's 'science fiction' fantasy, *Voyage to Venus*, as well
as being expressed more didactically in *The Problem of Pain.*

Granted, then, the necessity of this testing of Man's attitude to God,
of confronting the human race with the choice between God or self,
what significance should we attach to the fact that the forbidden fruit in
the *Genesis* story was "of the tree of the knowledge of good and evil"?

Simply this: knowledge of evil — and therefore of its contrast with goodness — could only be obtained in a perfect world by first bringing evil into *existence* through the sin of disobedience, and then suffering all its consequences. And since to sin against God involves cutting oneself off from the source of all life and of one's very being, disobedience could only lead to mental and physical corruption, ending in death. Hence there never was any question of unfallen Man having the option of "becoming wise" like God in some detached, painless, and 'academic' way, as the serpent (Satan) pretended when tempting Eve.

Once all this is understood, God's commandment to Adam and Eve *not* to eat the forbidden fruit can be seen to be what it always was: not only part of a necessary process of testing and perfecting Man's free will, but also a merciful prohibition intended for the protection and happiness of the human race. All of which is a far cry from the notion, nowhere even hinted at in the Bible, that there is something sinful about the pursuit of knowledge in the wider sense. Why else did God give us brains if not to explore the wonders of His creation?

At this point it is necessary — as Lewis realised — to deal with the scientific objection to the story and doctrine of the Fall, namely, that it is apparently contradicted by Darwinism. It is supposedly incompatible with the 'fact' of evolution.

Now before turning to Lewis's own answer to this objection, it needs to be emphasised — however offensive this may be to current secular sensibilities — that far from being a proven and unchallengeable 'fact', Darwinian evolution is actually only a *theory* about human origins which *may* be true but is also questioned by a number of biologists and scientists — not all of whom are Christians. Readers interested in the controversy between evolutionists and 'creationists' should turn to Appendix B, at the end of this book, for references to some of the literature on this subject. The only observation it is appropriate to make here is a methodological one: scientific knowledge is derived from the formulation and testing of theoretical hypotheses through observation and experiment, activities which can only be carried out by living human beings. Since modern scientists were not around at the time to witness the birth either of the Universe or of our solar system, or the beginnings of organic life, or the creation, appearance or development of animal species and the human race, their views about the remote past can at best only be intelligent guesses based on observations and infer-ences related to *current* physical, chemical, and biological processes. Whether, however, the structures and processes of Nature as we observe them today were once different, or were created and designed by God, are ultimately *philosophical* rather than scientific questions — though scientific observation may furnish useful hints or clues which may help to answer these questions (assuming they can be answered). For these reasons, it is dangerously misleading to pretend that science has either proved or disproved the theory of evolution or the alternative religious hypothesis of 'special creation'. Whilst there may or may not be apparently compelling scientific evidence for either view, *interpretation* of the relevant physical and chemical data is inevitably influenced (or distorted) by prior (if often unstated) philosophical or religious assumptions, and we need to be aware of this fact. Hence, for instance, if we are already convinced on philosophical grounds that there is no God, or that His existence is extremely improbable, we are more likely to believe in the truthfulness of Darwinism since it is difficult to imagine any alternative naturalistic explanation of the development of life and the appearance of complexity and apparent 'design' in Nature. On the other hand, if we believe in God and the truthfulness of the Bible, and adopt a literal rather than a metaphorical or allegorical interpretation of *Genesis*, we will look at the relevant scientific data through 'creationist' spectacles and seek confirmation of a truth in which we already believe on religious grounds.

What this means, therefore, is that if we want to restrict ourselves to a genuinely open-minded scientific approach, great care must be taken to distinguish between what the 'raw' field data actually and in itself reveals about the origins and development of life, and the conclusions that follow from fitting this data into a particular interpretive framework (whether Darwinian or 'creationist').

For example, take the extraordinarily complex structure of the human eye. A 'creationist' who believes in the existence of God and interprets *Genesis* literally, will regard its apparently perfectly designed structure as evidence that Man did not evolve from a jelly fish by a random and accidental process of chance mutations interacting with natural selection, but was directly created by God as a distinct species from the very beginning. An atheistical Darwinist, however, must necessarily take the opposite view, insisting that the human eye must have evolved, even if there is controversy about the precise *mechanism* of evolution. A believer in *theistic evolution*, on the other hand, whilst accepting the Darwinian hypothesis that the human eye evolved, will argue that its marvellously intricate structure, perfectly organised and adapted to produce vision, points to the existence of God as the creative and guiding force *behind* evolution, which has only been able to produce complex plants and animals from small and simple beginnings because it has been designed to do so by God. The alternative hypothesis, that the course of evolution is the product of blind chance, he will dismiss as being no more credible than the notion that the Oxford Dictionary was produced by an explosion in a printing works. Finally, let us imagine an open-minded and totally agnostic scientist (perhaps a rare being) who is neither an atheist nor a Christian, and is unencumbered by any religious or philosophical presuppositions except for a belief in the intelligibility of Nature and the possibility of discovering and framing scientific laws. *He* concludes that since it is difficult (as Darwin himself admitted) to explain how the human eye evolved, and there is also no conclusive *scientific* proof of the existence of God (no-one has seen Him through a telescope) the existence and development of the human eye (and similarly complex structures) remains a mystery which the progress of science has not yet unravelled.

Does this parable, and the arguments which preceded it, not suggest that sceptics ought to be careful before dismissing the story of the Fall of Man as 'unscientific'?

C. S. Lewis, as far as one can tell from his writings, did not reject Darwinism understood as a purely biological theory describing the mechanism by which God gradually created animals and the human race over a long period. But he was aware of the lack of confidence of some Darwinists in the empirical and theoretical foundations of their theory, hence his reference in a wartime Oxford Socratic Society paper to Professor D.M.S. Watson's 1943 statement that evolution was not accepted by zoologists "because it has been observed to occur or ... can be proved by logically coherent evidence to be true" but because of a philosophical prejudice against the alternative concept of "special creation", regarded as "clearly incredible". However, wisely avoiding entanglement in a scientific controversy which he evidently did not feel qualified to participate in, Lewis insisted that there were no sound reasons for rejecting the doctrine of the Fall on scientific grounds, even if the theory of evolution were true.

> Prehistoric man, because he is prehistoric, is known to us only by the material things he made — or rather by a chance selection from among the more durable things he made. It is not the fault of archaeologists that they have no better evidence: but this penury constitutes a continual temptation to infer more than we have any right to infer, to assume that the community which made the superior artefacts was superior in all respects... The very same pot which would prove its maker a genius if it were the first pot ever made in the world, would prove its maker a dunce if it came after millenniums of pot-making. The whole modern estimate of primitive man is based upon that idolatry of artefacts which is a great corporate sin of our own civilisation. We forget that our prehistoric ancestors made all the useful discoveries, except that of chloroform, which have ever been made. To them we owe language, the family, clothing, the use of fire, the domestication of animals, the wheel, the ship, poetry and agriculture. Science, then, has nothing to say for or against the doctrine of the Fall. (*The Problem of Pain*, pp. 58-9.)

Having dismissed the misconception that modern science contradicts the doctrine of the Fall, Lewis offers his own interpretation of both this event and the consciousness of Paradisal Man, demonstrating in the process the compatibility of his interpretation with all that we know about history, the human heart, and the remote past.

> I do not doubt that if the Paradisal man could now appear among us, we should regard him as an utter savage, a creature to be exploited or, at best, patronised. Only one or two, and those the holiest among us, would glance a second time at the naked, shaggy-bearded, slowspoken creature: but they, after a few minutes, would fall at his feet.
>
> We do not know how many of these creatures God made, nor how long they continued in the Paradisal state. But sooner or later they fell. Someone or something whispered that they could become as gods — that they could cease directing their lives to their Creator... They wanted, as we say, to 'call their souls their own '. But that means to live a lie, for our souls are not in fact, our own. They wanted some corner in the universe of which they could say to God, 'This is our business, not yours.' But there is no such corner. They wanted to be

nouns, but they were, and eternally must be, mere adjectives... The
process was not, I conceive, comparable to mere deterioration as it
may now occur in a human individual; it was a loss of status as a
species. What man lost by the Fall was his original specific nature.
'Dust thou art, and unto dust shalt thou return.' (*The Problem of Pain*,
pp. 63-5.)

The ultimate consequence, in short, of that turning away from God to
self which constitutes the basic sin behind the Fall, was physical and
spiritual death following Man's inevitable separation from God — the
source of his life and being. The result in social terms? Nearly all that
we call human history: poverty, ambition, war, prostitution, classes,
empires, tyranny and slavery.

The idea of the Fall, and of inherited 'original sin', is naturally repugnant to modern man's pride, just as the Judeo-Christian concept of
God is resented by those who dislike the notion that there may be an
eternal sanction behind the Moral Law they violate in the pursuit of
power and pleasure. Nevertheless, the daily and historical evidence of
the reality of 'original sin' is overwhelming. Even leaving aside the
degree to which history is, as Lewis stressed, largely a record of man's
inhumanity to man, we know from our own relationships and internal
experience the extent to which our lives are marred by self-centredness.

If, for all these reasons, the Biblical doctrine of the Fall seems credible, what about the perennially thorny problem of unjust suffering?
Even if we accept the truth that pain and death may be the natural consequence and just penalty of sin, how can the existence and goodness of
God be reconciled with the terrible fact that suffering so often afflicts
the *innocent*? Would God — if He really exists — allow babies to die
of AIDS, or let children be sexually abused and murdered? And what
about the innocent victims of drunken drivers and natural disasters, like
forest fires and earthquakes?

The lack of correspondence between individual desert and personal
suffering in this life is indeed only part of a wider picture of a world in
which injustice frequently prevails and social and material success only
too often bears little relation to personal merit. Yet why should this be
thought to constitute a definitive argument against God's existence or
goodness? It may seem a plausible objection to theism and Christianity,

and great thinkers like John Stuart Mill certainly found it convincing, but its superficial character is highlighted by two interesting facts: the problem of unjust suffering, far from being an embarrassing phenomenon glossed over by Christian (and Jewish) writers, is one of the central themes of the Bible and is frequently mentioned (especially in the Psalms) in precisely those passages which *affirm* God's goodness and love; secondly, as C. S. Lewis pointed out, some of the most powerful affirmations of the reality and goodness of God have been written in the midst of suffering — by Boethius, for example, on the eve of being beaten to death, and by Augustine contemplating the sack of Rome. Were these Biblical and early Christian writers simply misguided or did they perceive truths that have escaped the attention of unbelieving critics like Voltaire, Shelley, Russell and Mill?

As we saw when examining Lewis's reasons for rejecting atheism, moral arguments against the existence and goodness of God are ultimately self-contradictory since they presuppose a moral law or standard whose existence cannot be explained or accounted for on non-theistic premises. But there is an additional reason for rejecting the belief that unjust suffering contradicts the notion that God's sovereign goodness presides over Nature and human destinies. The suffering of the innocent is a necessary consequence of the misuse of free will, and an inevitable result of the Fall.

Like all orthodox Christians, Lewis accepted the Biblical view that the entry of sin into the world — both human and angelic — damaged creation and the whole natural order, with all those results in terms of disease, natural disasters, sickness and death that have become so dreadfully familiar to us. But what he chiefly stressed in his discussion of innocent suffering in *The Problem of Pain*, was the degree to which God's hands are voluntarily tied by His gift of free will to Man. This imposes limitations on His ability to interfere with human behaviour and its consequences. As the following passage makes clear, God cannot prevent human beings from harming each other without effectively abolishing free will:

> We can, perhaps, conceive of a world in which God corrected the results of this abuse of free-will by His creatures at every moment: so that a wooden beam became soft as grass when it was used as a weapon,

and the air refused to obey me if I attempted to set up in it the sound-waves that carry lies or insults. But such a world would be one in which wrong actions were impossible, and in which, therefore, freedom of the will would be void... That God can and does, on occasions, modify the behaviour of matter and produce what we call miracles, is part of Christian faith; but the very conception of a common, and therefore stable, world, demands that these occasions should be extremely rare... Try to exclude the possibility of suffering which the order of nature and the existence of free-wills involve, and you find that you have excluded life itself. (*The Problem of Pain*, p.27.)

It is only after people have faced and understood this bleak but necessary truth that they can begin to understand why the message of the Christian Gospel is one of 'good news' (which is, of course, the actual meaning of the word 'gospel'). It brings 'good news' because it affirms that far from leaving humanity in the lurch to bear the full consequences of sin in time and eternity, God has visited our planet and in some strange but wonderful way redeemed the human race, not only making it possible for individuals to have a new relationship with God, but setting in motion the removal of evil and the restoration and recreation of the entire cosmos.

To do full justice to Lewis's interpretation of the great Christian doctrines of the Incarnation and the Atonement, and the life and claims of Christ, is not possible within the space of this short introductory study, but the following outline encapsulates the main features of the analysis contained in *Mere Christianity*, *Miracles*, and *The Problem of Pain*.

Since God is perfect and holy, He cannot — by His very nature — tolerate evil or endure its presence. As a result, fallen humanity is not only automatically cut off from Him, but is also under condemnation, since God's justice demands that the penalty of sin be paid in full. God's very goodness requires that sinful human beings must bear the full and logical consequences of having misused their free will to reject their Creator. And what are these consequences? That having voluntarily separated themselves from God — the source of all life — unredeemed human beings inevitably face the prospect not only of suffering in this life and physical death, but of the separation of their immortal souls from God in eternity. And since life without God means an eternity of

existence shorn of all hope, peace, love and joy, the Bible rightly portrays the condition of damnation as something indescribably terrible.

Christianity affirms, however, that God is Love, and because He is
Love, that He is merciful as well as just, and therefore unwilling — as
the Bible declares — "that any should perish" . Hence, from the very
moment of the Fall, God announced and began to carry out His plan of
salvation for mankind. And what did that plan entail? Lewis gives the
best brief summary of his answer to this question in *Mere Christianity*.

> First of all He left us conscience, the sense of right and wrong: and all
> through history there have been people trying (some of them very hard)
> to obey it. None of them ever quite succeeded. Secondly, He sent the
> human race what I call good dreams: I mean those queer stories scat-
> tered all through the heathen religions about a god who dies and comes
> to life again and, by his death, has somehow given new life to men.
> Thirdly, He selected one particular people and spent several centuries
> hammering into their heads the sort of God He was — that there was
> only one of Him and that He cared about right conduct. Those people
> were the Jews, and the Old Testament gives an account of the ham-
> mering process.
>
> Then comes the real shock. Among these Jews there suddenly turns
> up a man who goes about talking as if He was God. He claims to
> forgive sins. He says He has always existed. He says He is coming to
> judge the world at the end of time. Now let us get this clear. Among
> Pantheists, like the Indians, anyone might say that he was a part of
> God, or one with God: there would be nothing very odd about it. But
> this man, since He was a Jew, could not mean that kind of God. God,
> in their language, meant the Being outside the world, who had made
> it and was infinitely different from anything else. And when you have
> grasped that, you will see that what this man said was quite simply the
> most shocking thing that has ever been uttered by human lips. (*Mere
> Christianity*, p.51.)

Lewis's reference here to Christ, and his subsequent defence of Jesus's
claims to Divinity, will be discussed shortly when looking at some of the
objections commonly raised against the truthfulness of the Gospels and
the New Testament, but at this point we are merely concerned with out-
lining the purpose of the Incarnation — with understanding the reason
why God became Man; *why* God the Son (The Second Person of the

Trinity) not only took on our human flesh and lived amongst us two thousand years ago, but also suffered, died, and came back to life, and by doing so, somehow atoned for our sins and restored our broken relationship with God. However, before tackling this great subject, one thing must first be clarified.

Christians, Lewis pointed out, can interpret the Incarnation and the Atonement in different ways, for it is in one sense an awesome mystery which human reason and imagination cannot wholly fathom, and which can be looked at from different angles. But what is important and common to all Christians, he argued, is their assertion of the *fact* of the Incarnation and Atonement — that through the actual life, death and resurrection of Jesus, God has indeed reconciled us to Himself and given us an eternal victory over sin and death. Those, therefore, who believe in the 'good news' of the Gospel and give their ransomed lives to Christ, can save their souls regardless of whether or not they can fully understand or explain how this process of salvation works. To use the analogy Lewis employs in *Mere Christianity*, we can enjoy the benefits of salvation in the same way as our bodies can be nourished by food whether or not we know anything about vitamins.

Given, nevertheless, the existence and reality of God, and that Christian faith, *pace* Pascal, ought therefore to be a leap into the light, it is important to try and understand as much as we can about the Incarnation and the Atonement, and Lewis's views on these matters. And the key to understanding lies in the consideration of one central question: what was the *one* thing God had to do to save Man which only *He* could do, and which only He could do by uniting His divine nature with human nature?

To put it simply: He had to find a way of reconciling His justice with His mercy so that the penalty for human sin — separation from God and eternal death — could be paid in full *without* it involving the final destruction of humanity. Having originally created us with free wills, so that we could be voluntarily and blissfully united with Him (and each other) in love, God could not undo the effects of the Fall merely by annulling its consequences or arresting the progress of sin and decay, as if life were a game whose rules could be arbitrarily changed to suit the convenience of the players. To do so, Lewis argued:

would have been to decline the problem which God had set Himself when He created the world, the problem of expressing His goodness through the total drama of a world containing free agents, in spite of, and by means of, their rebellion against Him   (*The Problem of Pain*, pp. 66-7.)

On the other hand, God's love could not rest in the knowledge that the human creatures He had made were doomed to destruction, and could never, given their sinful condition, be reunited with Him by their own efforts. Hence there was only one solution, only one way in which God could knock down the wall of separation erected by the Fall: by Himself becoming Man so that He could die, and by dying, pay off that debt incurred by human sin which no ordinary human being could pay. It is as if God, as the judge in a court case, had to fine his son for a particular offence, but having passed sentence and therefore performed his duty as a judge to uphold the law, had then taken off his judge's robes and — as the boy's father — paid the fine himself. In other words, the whole point of the Incarnation and Atonement is that only as Man could Christ (God) die, but as *God* He could overcome sin and death and bestow upon redeemed men and women the gift of everlasting life. That is why, as the Gospels describe, the death of Jesus was followed by His resurrection — an event He Himself predicted when He was preparing His bewildered disciples for His arrest, trial, and crucifixion.

Lewis, like all orthodox Christians, affirmed these great central truths about the Incarnation and the Atonement, but the angle from which he looked at these truths and interpreted them revolved around the theme of repentance. The way he puts it in *Mere Christianity*, is that Jesus came into the world to help us die to sin and live for God by restoring our relationship with our Creator through His death and resurrection. Referring to the Fall, Lewis begins his explanation by pointing out that fallen man is not simply an imperfect creature who needs improvement, but a rebel who must surrender his arms and abandon his attempt to live as if he belonged to himself rather than to God. Such a surrender, however, involves more than simply saying sorry and eating humble pie. Proper repentance means unlearning all the self-conceit and self-will that human beings have been training themselves into for centuries. But since this means killing part of yourself, undergoing a kind of death, it needs a *good* person to repent — someone honest and brave enough to admit his fallen spiritual condition and need for God's forgiveness. But here comes the catch: only a bad person needs to repent but only a good person can repent perfectly. The worse you are, the more you need to repent and the less you can do it.

> Can we do it if God helps us?... suppose our human nature which can suffer and die was amalgamated with God's nature in one person — then that person could help us. He could surrender His will, and suffer and die, because He was man; and He could do it perfectly because He was God. You and I can go through this process only if God does it in us; but God can do it only if He becomes man. Our attempts at this dying will succeed only if we men share in God's dying, just as our thinking can succeed only because it is a drop out of the ocean of His intelligence: but we cannot share God's dying unless God dies; and He cannot die except by being a man. That is the sense in which He pays our debt, and suffers for us what He Himself need not suffer at all. (*Mere Christianity*, pp. 56-7.)

Having examined the core of the Christian Gospel, and Lewis's interpretation of it, we come to the whole question of Christian morality and the nature of the Christian life. How should the redemptive work of Christ be manifest in our lives? What does it mean to say that we have 'new life in Christ', and how does it affect human relationships and our outlook on the world? What exactly *is* Christian love? Is the Christian understanding of morality radically opposed to all other systems of morality?

Whole books could be written in answer to each of these questions, and much of Lewis's writing covers this ground, but again there is only space here for some brief comments about Lewis's discussion of these matters if we are to do justice to his defence of the truth of Christianity against some of the standard objections brought against it by atheists and other critics.

Those interested in a full examination of Lewis's views about Christian ethics, the nature of the Christian life, and Christianity and culture, must read his books and collected essays — especially the later chapters of *Mere Christianity*, *Christian Reflections*, *The Four Loves*, *Undeceptions: Essays on Theology And Ethics*, *The Abolition of Man*, and *Letters To Malcolm, Chiefly About Prayer*. Some of these matters are also briefly touched upon in the next chapter, which discusses Lewis's political and cultural Conservatism. The relevant point to make here is that Lewis rightly argued that what distinguishes Christianity from other religious and philosophical systems is not so much its moral teaching, but its triumphant assertion that God has entered history, and having done so, has not only redeemed mankind but can actually help men and women to lead new and better lives in the present.

Christianity also promises, the Bible reveals, that the day will come when evil will finally be destroyed by the return of Christ as King and Judge, at the end of history. Until then, however, the New Testament emphasises that Christians are called upon to be 'salt and light' in the world and 'Christ's ambassadors', and as such, to do good, fight evil, and share God's love and the 'good news' of the Gospel with their fellow human beings. And to do all this, Lewis explained, they must not only give their lives to Christ, but must allow the spirit and life of Christ to flow into them and operate through them — both individually and collectively. Only by being in touch with God and open to the flow of His power and love through faith, the study of the Bible, prayer, and the sacraments, can we obtain the help we need to live upright lives, overcome evil, and serve others. Hence, wrote Lewis:

> ... the Christian is in a different position from other people who are trying to be good. They hope, by being good, to please God if there is one; or — if they think there is not — at least they hope to deserve approval from good men. But the Christian thinks any good he does comes from the Christ-life inside him. He does not think God will love us because we are good, but that God will make us good because He loves us; just as the roof of a greenhouse does not attract the sun because it is bright, but becomes bright because the sun shines on it. (*Mere Christianity*, p.61.)

This means, said Lewis, that a Christian is not a person who never goes wrong, but a person who is enabled to repent and pick himself up and begin over again after each fall — because the Christ-life is inside him repairing him all the time.

Christians also believe that God helps us even to pray — to engage

in the very act of speaking and listening to Him. As Lewis put it, returning to the theme of the Trinity and the particular role of the Third Person
in God (the Holy Spirit):

> An ordinary simple Christian kneels down to say his prayers... God is
> the thing to which he is praying — the goal he is trying to reach. God
> is also the thing inside him which is pushing him on — the motive
> power. God is also the road or bridge along which he is being pushed
> to that goal. So that the whole threefold life of the three-personal Be-
> ing is actually going on in that ordinary little bedroom where an ordi-
> nary man is saying his prayers. The man is being caught up into the
> higher kind of life — what I called *Zoe* or spiritual life: he is being
> pulled into God, by God, while still remaining himself. (*Mere Chris-
> tianity*, p. 139.)

This brings us to the ultimate question: what is the *final* goal of the
Christian life? What is it that God is trying to do with and inside each
one of us? The Christian answer, according to Lewis, is startling but
simple. Having restored our broken relationship with Him and redeemed
us from the consequences of Original Sin, God is intent on nothing less
than recreating our characters and personalities so that whilst remaining the distinct and unique individuals He always intended us to be, we
become perfect mirrors of His beauty, love and goodness — little Christs,
if you like, freed from every flaw and imperfection, and able to share the
love and life of God in a recreated Universe no longer marred by death,
sorrow, or sin. That is the prospect held out to us in the New Testament,
but the road to it is hard and stony, for although the most difficult part
of the journey — the act of atonement — has been traversed for us by
Christ, the process of sanctification (of being remade in God's likeness)
is painful. It involves a lifelong struggle against self-centredness, self-
will, and our whole fallen condition — an internal battle fought out in
the midst of trials and sorrows which are not only inseparable from life
in our damaged and fallen world, but which create the pressures which
challenge and improve our characters if we respond to them in the right
way. God, wrote Lewis, will change us on the inside if we let Him, and
will constantly forgive our mistakes and sins as we bring them to Him
each day in repentance, but He will be satisfied with nothing less in the
end than absolute perfection. And the reason for this lies precisely in

the fact that He is Love:

> To ask that God's love should be content with us as we are is to ask that God should cease to be God: because He is what He is, His love must, in the nature of things, be impeded and repelled by certain stains in our present character, and because He already loves us He must labour to make us lovable. We cannot even wish, in our better moments, that He could reconcile Himself to our present impurities... What we would here and now call our "happiness" is not the end God chiefly has in view: but when we are such as He can love without impediment, we shall in fact be happy. (*The Problem of Pain*, p.39.)

It is easy, of course, to resent the idea that we need to be remade, and to dislike the conception of God it entails, but if God exists and is our loving Creator, and our nature is what we all (in our honest moments) know it to be, our resentment is irrational and merely symptomatic of our fallen spiritual condition. In that sense, said Lewis, we are rather like a dog, with smells and habits which frustrate man's love and move him to wash it, house-train it, and teach it not to steal:

> To the puppy the whole proceeding would seem, if it were a theologian, to cast grave doubts on the 'goodness' of man: but the full-grown and full-trained dog, larger, healthier, and longer-lived than the wild dog, and admitted, as it were by Grace, to a whole world of affections, loyalties, interests, and comforts entirely beyond its animal destiny, would have no such doubts. (*The Problem of Pain*, p.35.)

There are those who will argue, at this stage, that it is one thing to demonstrate the plausibility of Christianity as a religion which explains the human condition and describes the way in which God may have dealt with the problem of evil — including the need to redeem and refashion corrupted human nature. It is quite another thing to demonstrate convincingly that its affirmations about the Incarnation and Atonement are historically *true*. How do we know that Jesus was the 'Son of God', or — to be theologically rigorous — 'God the Son Incarnate'? Can we rely on the evidence of the Gospels?

One objection to the whole notion of the Incarnation is a peculiarly modern one, and stems from our seemingly greater awareness in the twentieth century of the vastness of the Universe and the apparent insignificance, by comparison, of Man and the Earth he inhabits. Hence, it is argued, the Christian story is suspect, since the idea that God not only loves us but has uniquely favoured the human race with a redemptive visit to our planet, obviously reflects an ignorant and outdated geocentric view of the Cosmos. Furthermore, the Universe may well contain other inhabited planets and intelligent life-forms, which makes the assumptions underlying Christianity look even more ridiculous.

Appearances, however, are deceptive, and C.S. Lewis is particularly effective in exposing the superficiality of these contemporary objections to the Christian Gospel — notably in *Miracles* (in 'A Chapter of Red Herrings') and in his essay on 'Religion and Rocketry' in the collection entitled *Fern-Seed and Elephants*.

The first point he makes is that the immensity of the Universe is not a new discovery but was known in ancient times, and therefore hardly constitutes a dramatic new piece of evidence against Christianity. Not only did Ptolemy reveal, more than seventeen hundred years ago, that in relation to the distance of the fixed stars the whole Earth must be regarded as a point with no magnitude, but his astronomical system was universally accepted in the Dark and Middle Ages. Hence the insignificance of the Earth was a commonplace to Boethius, King Alfred, Dante and Chaucer:

> The real question is quite different from what we commonly suppose. The real question is why the spatial insignificance of Earth, after being asserted by Christian philosophers, sung by Christian poets, and commented on by Christian moralists for some fifteen centuries, without the slightest suspicion that it conflicted with their theology, should suddenly in quite modern times have been set up as a stock argument against Christianity and enjoyed, in that capacity, a brilliant career. (*Miracles*, p.53.)

The reason, suggested Lewis, lies in the false assumptions people make about the kind of Universe implied by Christianity. In the first place, they assume that there is some sort of connection between size and significance, but whilst this may be psychologically understandable ("we all *feel* the incongruity of supposing, say, that the planet Earth might be more important than the Great Nebula in Andromeda."), it is clearly illogical and fallacious. Is a horse more important than a man, or a leg than a brain? Secondly, the critics implicitly assume that the Incarnation implies some particular merit in Man which moves God to take special measures to rescue him; but this, of course, is nonsense, and misses the whole point of the Christian Gospel: "Christ did not die for men because they were intrinsically worth dying for, but because He is intrinsically love, and therefore loves infinitely." (*Miracles*, p.52) It is because we are fallen and therefore, in a sense, not worth dying for, that God visited our planet, just as it is the one 'lost sheep' the Good Shepherd seeks — in Jesus's famous parable — not the ninety-nine righteous ones who never strayed.

As for the problem supposedly posed by the possible existence of other intelligent species, it too melts away on closer examination:

> The sceptic asks how we can believe that God so 'came down' to this one tiny planet. The question would be embarrassing if we knew (1) that there are rational creatures on any of the other bodies that float in space; (2) that they have, like us, fallen and need redemption; (3) that their redemption must be in the same mode as ours; (4) that redemption in this mode has been withheld from them. But we know none of them. The universe may be full of happy lives that never needed redemption. It may be full of lives that have been redeemed in modes suitable to their condition of which we can form no conception. It may be full of lives that have been redeemed in the very same mode as our own. It may be full of things quite other than life in which God is interested though we are not. (*Miracles*, pp. 55-6.)

The compatibility of Christianity with the existence of other species of intelligent life on other planets is, in fact, the theme of two of C. S. Lewis's science fiction fantasies, *Out of the Silent Planet* and *Voyage to Venus*, and will be further discussed in the final chapter dealing with the fictional treatment of Lewis's ideas. The point to emphasise here is that the emptiness of 'modern' cosmological arguments against Christianity is highlighted by their very tendency to contradict each other.

> If the universe is teeming with life other than ours, then this, we are told, makes it quite ridiculous to believe that God should be so concerned with the human race as to 'come down from Heaven' and be

made man for its redemption. If, on the other hand, our planet is really unique in harbouring organic life, then this is thought to prove that life is only an accidental by-product in the universe and so again to disprove our religion. We treat God as the policeman in the story treated the suspect; whatever he does 'will be used in evidence against Him.' (*Miracles*, p.54.)

Honest and thoughtful critics of Christianity might agree that Lewis successfully disposes of the above-mentioned 'scientific' red herrings, and they might even acknowledge the plausibility and credibility of his speculations about God's possible dealings with other intelligent species — if these exist. But as everyone knows, the most common objection to the story of Jesus presented in the Gospels is that these narratives contain descriptions of miracles supposedly performed by or involving Jesus, and since the occurrence of miracles is regarded as an impossibility on scientific grounds, the Gospel writers are either dismissed as unreliable witnesses whose understanding was distorted by their ignorance of the laws of nature, or they are attacked as liars and propagandists. More charitable critics — particularly modern liberal theologians — argue that the Gospels are not based on eye witness accounts of Jesus's life at all, but were written much later and should be regarded as an expression of the faith and theology of the early Church, the truths they contain being merely symbolical and allegorical rather than historical.

Against these objections and assumptions Lewis levelled some of his most formidable intellectual artillery — principally (again) in *Miracles*, but also in a witty theological paper originally presented to Cambridge students in May 1959, and published in *Christian Reflections* and *Fernseed and Elephants* — under the title, 'Modern Theology and Biblical Criticism'. They merit close and detailed study by those who imagine that orthodox Christianity has been refuted by modern science and biblical scholarship.

Lewis's counter-attack on the critics of the Gospel story and the claims of Christ is many-sided, but three strands of argument stand out as particularly relevant and worthy of examination.

First of all, Lewis points out, the belief that miracles are intrinsically improbable cannot be supported on scientific grounds since the assumption on which scientific reasoning is based — that Nature and her laws are uniform — is not based on (or provable by) experience, but is in fact an *a priori* philosophical assumption which can only be justified on theistic premises, and since these premises reveal the existence of God as the Power or Being who created and sustains the Universe, miracles cannot be ruled out since there is nothing to prevent God suspending or interfering with laws of His own creation.

As Lewis explains in his critique of Hume's famous sceptical *Essay on Miracles*, the assertion that the uniformity of Nature rules out miracles, involves a process of unprovable circular reasoning since the conclusion of the argument is already contained in its premise. By saying that Nature is uniform, sceptics like Hume merely mean that ordinary scientific laws are never suspended or interrupted, which is, of course, the same thing as saying from the outset, without any investigation, that miracles have indeed never occurred. Similarly, the belief that Nature is uniform — that natural laws do not vary across space or time — cannot be the product of experience since the principle of uniformity has first to be assumed before experience can prove anything. Unless we *already* know that Nature always behaves in the same way, the fact that a thing has happened a billion times before does not make it any more probable that it will happen again.

Not only, then, does the scientific case against miracles beg the question, but as we have already indicated in the earlier discussion of atheism, our very confidence in the orderliness of Nature stems from the fact that she is God's creation:

> Professor Whitehead points out that centuries of belief in a God who combined "the personal energy of Jehovah" with "the rationality of a Greek philosopher" first produced that firm expectation of systematic order which rendered possible the birth of modern science. Men became scientific because they expected Law in Nature, and they expected Law in Nature because they believed in a Legislator. (*Miracles*, p.110.)

The implication of this analysis is that on theistic premises it is possible both to affirm the normal uniformitarian course of Nature *and* to allow for the possibility of miracles should God choose to perform them, and this is in fact the attitude of the Gospel writers and of Jesus's contemporaries. Far from being ignorant of ordinary scientific laws, the very fact that they regarded certain events as miracles clearly demonstrates that they understood these to be an interruption of the ordinary course of Nature. Otherwise, why else are we told in the Gospels that Joseph was minded to break off his engagement to Mary when he learnt that she was pregnant with Jesus? He knew as well as we do that conception is usually the result of sexual intercourse. Hence, Lewis concludes:

> The Being who threatens Nature's claim to omnipotence confirms her in her lawful occasions. Give us this ha'porth of tar and we will save the ship. The alternative is really much worse. Try to make Nature absolute and you find that her uniformity is not even probable. By claiming too much, you get nothing. You get the deadlock, as in Hume. Theology offers you a working arrangement, which leaves the scientist free to continue his experiments and the Christian to continue his prayers. (*Miracles*, p.110.)

Having demonstrated the possibility of miracles and countered the scientific prejudice that otherwise prevents an open-minded investigation of the Gospel story, Lewis looks at the actual miracles recorded in the New Testament and argues that far from them being the sort of arbitrary supernatural events you read about in fairy tales, their character is consistent with what we know of God's nature and the way in which He normally operates in Creation. Instead of beasts turning into men, talking trees, or magic rings, we read, for example, of water turning into wine, or a few loaves and fishes feeding thousands, miracles which represent a speeding up and localisation of what usually occurs gradually and generally in Nature. What they tell us is that the God who created the Universe, and with it, the natural processes by which water and seedlings of wheat are annually turned into wine and bread with the co-operation of human labour, once short-circuited these processes and performed the same 'miracles' as Man in ancient Palestine:

> God creates the vine and teaches it to draw up water by its roots and, with the aid of the sun, to turn that water into a juice which will ferment and take on certain qualities. Thus every year, from Noah's time till ours, God turns water into wine. That, men fail to see. Either like the Pagans they refer the process to some finite spirit, Bacchus or Dionysus: or else, like the moderns, they attribute real and ultimate

causality to the chemical and other material phenomena which are all that our senses can discover in it. But when Christ at Cana makes water into wine, the mask is off. The miracle has only half its effect if it only convinces us that Christ is God: it will have its full effect if whenever we see a vineyard or drink a glass of wine we remember that here works He who sat at the wedding party in Cana...That same mysterious energy which we call gravitational when it steers the planets and biochemical when it heals a body is the efficient cause of all recoveries, and if God exists, that energy, directly or indirectly, is His. All who are cured are cured by Him, the healer within. But once He did it visibly, a Man meeting a man. (*Undeceptions*, pp. 9-10.)

One of the chief purposes, in other words, of Christ's miracles, argued Lewis, is that by revealing in close up and on a small scale what God is always doing on a larger scale in Nature, they bear witness to the divinity of Jesus — to the fact that God, our King and Creator, once moved and dwelt amongst us. Other miracles, like the Virgin Birth and the Resurrection, whilst also representing in miniature God's larger creative activity (as the author of life, sex, and the renewal of Spring), testify to the Divinity of Jesus in a more direct and dramatic sense, but in a way which is still comprehensible to our reason. Hence the story of the Virgin Birth may seem shocking in a scientific age, but we can see, after a moment's reflection, that only a virginal conception brought about by the Spirit of God without the agency of a fallen human father could serve as the vehicle for the creation of the sinless Man who was to be the Saviour of mankind. We ought similarly to be able to grasp the point that since only the Eternal Self-existent Being could conquer death, the Resurrection of Jesus (assuming it occurred) confirms that He was (and is) the Incarnate God. As Lewis put it, where else but in uncreated light can the darkness be swallowed up?

But these observations bring us face to face with those sceptics who doubt the historical authenticity and truthfulness of the Gospels. 'It is all very well', these critics will argue, 'to demonstrate the possibility of miracles and their consistency with Christian doctrine and theistic truth, but what reason have we for believing that the account we read in the Gospels of the life and work of Jesus is accurate, and that all these miracles actually happened?'

The answer is that there are many excellent reasons for doing so, and the first one is that most of the historical scepticism about the Gospels displayed by modernist scholars and critics is not rooted in a thorough and open-minded study of the Gospel narratives, but is the expression of precisely that prejudice against the supernatural which we have just examined. What usually happens, Lewis points out, is that these critics start out with the conviction that miracles cannot or do not occur, and as a result, they either dismiss all the miracle stories recorded in the Gospels as complete fabrications; or they reinterpret them allegorically; or they dream up the most fanciful and unlikely 'natural' explanations for the events they describe. Another alternative is to engage in elaborate historical reconstructions about the origin of particular stories in order to explain away and thereby eliminate the supernatural element in them — as happens, for instance, when Gospel passages containing prophecies which came true are alleged to have been written *after* the events they supposedly anticipated!

This, again, is not the place to enter into a detailed analysis of the scholarly debate about the reliability of the New Testament (and, indeed, of the Bible in general): the important point that Lewis is making is simply that the *philosophical* presuppositions of the biblical critics must be taken into account when assessing the credibility of their attacks on the Gospels. This is particularly relevant, for instance, to the whole controversy about the reliability of the Resurrection narratives.

If we remain genuinely open-minded about the possible existence of God and the possibility of miracles, our approach to these purported eye-witness accounts of the appearances of the Risen Christ to His disciples will be one of open-ended inquiry. If, on the other hand, we begin by ruling out all possibility that Jesus might have actually risen from the dead, we will be forced to prefer any 'natural' explanation of the fact of the Empty Tomb, however far-fetched. Hence, for example, all those implausible theories that have long been current among the Gospel critics to explain away the embarrassing historical fact that the enemies of the Early Church were unable to deny the disappearance of the body of Jesus. If the official Jewish and Roman authorities *had* been able to do so, by producing His dead body, Christianity would have been killed off in its infancy, but since this didn't happen, the sceptics have been forced to come up with their own unconvincing explanations for the Empty Tomb.

The three most popular ones are that (1) the disciples stole the body to create the Resurrection myth (2) Jesus did not die from his wounds on the Cross but recovered in the tomb and subsequently appeared to His followers, convincing them of His Resurrection and Divinity. And (3) the disciples were the victims of collective hallucination. Yet are we really to believe that any of these 'natural' explanations is more probable than the supernatural one recorded in the New Testament? Is it likely that Jesus's terrified and demoralised followers, who had fled at His arrest and been shattered by His execution, would have found the courage, motivation and strength to overcome the Roman soldiers guarding the Tomb and steal the body of their dead Master? Is it likely, having done so, that they would have endured persecution and martyrdom for what they knew to be a lie? Is it imaginable that Jesus could have survived the appalling rigours of a Roman crucifixion and then, in his wounded and weakened state, rolled away, unaided, the huge stone sealing his tomb, and having overpowered the Roman guards, made his escape? Would the disciples have been likely to mistake this half dead broken figure tottering into their midst, as their Risen Lord, the triumphant Conqueror of sin and death? And what is the likelihood that a group of frightened and disappointed men, convinced of the ruin of their messianic hopes, would have had encouraging hallucinations involving a Risen Jesus — particularly given the fact that the Gospels emphatically record that most of Jesus's disciples refused, at first, to believe in His Resurrection? Do hallucinations, moreover, normally affect many people at once, or recur on separate occasions over a specific period of 40 days after which they abruptly cease?

One has only to begin considering these questions to appreciate the force of Lewis's warning about the absurdities to which modernist critics and liberal theologians are led by their failure to free themselves from arbitrary philosophical preconceptions about the supernatural. If, however, this prejudice is suspended when examining the Gospels, what can we learn about their reliability from an examination of the relevant texts? What does the *internal* evidence tell us about the trustworthiness of the Gospel writers?

Before looking at C. S. Lewis's answers to these questions, one point needs to be stressed at the outset. If the possibility of God's existence and the miraculous is accepted, there is no good reason for treating the

Gospel narratives as inherently less reliable than any other ancient text. If we feel justified in relying on Caesar's *Gallic Wars* for much of our knowledge of ancient Gaul, we should be equally willing to consider the possibility that the Gospel writers give us an accurate picture of the life, personality, and miracles of Jesus, particularly given the undoubted fact that we have more information about Jesus than about any other figure of ancient history. Apart from the voluminous witness of the New Testament (whose manuscript evidence is earlier and more plentiful than that for Caesar's *Gallic Wars*), the historicity of Jesus is also confirmed by non-Christian writers, such as Josephus (a Jewish contemporary), and Roman historians like Tacitus and Suetonius. Archaeological evidence has also, in recent years, confirmed the historical accuracy of many of the details in Luke's Gospel. Furthermore, the most recent biblical scholarship suggests that the Gospels were written down well within the lifetime of Jesus's followers and contemporaries, and it is therefore at least arguable that if they contained serious errors, these would not have survived unchallenged and uncorrected. The very opening words of Luke's Gospel emphasise the centrality of eye witness testimony to the Gospel story:

> In as much as many have undertaken to compile a narrative of the things which have been accomplished among us, just as they were delivered to us by those who from the beginning were eyewitnesses and ministers of the word, it seemed good to me also, having followed all things closely for some time past, to write an orderly account for you, most excellent Theophilus, that you may know the truth concerning the things of which you have been informed. (*Luke* 1:1-4.)

Turning, then, to the Gospels themselves, what is the answer to the assertion of modernist liberal scholars that they do not give us a true picture of the historical Jesus but merely tell us about the faith and beliefs of the Early Church? What was Lewis's response to this attack on orthodox Christianity?

One way of responding is by pointing out that the honesty and truthfulness of the Gospel writers is suggested by the significant fact that they do not hesitate to record events which reveal Jesus's disciples (and therefore the first great leaders of the Christian Church) in a poor light. To give only some of the most famous examples: the Gospels record the disciples quarrelling about which of them will be first in the Kingdom of Heaven; they reveal Peter's denial of Jesus after His arrest, and the fact that all the disciples deserted Him in His hour of need; they record 'Doubting Thomas's' refusal to believe in His resurrection, and several instances of Jesus rebuking His disciples for their lack of faith and understanding. Indeed, the bewilderment of the disciples at many of Jesus's sayings — particularly His warnings about His impending arrest and execution — is a theme running through the whole of the Gospels. Are these accounts of human error, sin, foolishness and weakness, the usual stuff of propaganda? Would propagandist writers record their Hero crying out on the Cross: "My God, my God, why has thou forsaken me?" (*Matthew* 27:46, and *Mark* 15:34)?

Equally interesting, however, are all those details in the Gospels, all those vivid pictures of encounters and conversations, which, as Lewis insisted, have the 'ring of truth' about them to anyone trained and experienced in literary analysis. In developing this argument, Lewis begins by challenging the narrow expertise of many professional Biblical critics, illustrating his case from one of these critics, who writes that the Fourth Gospel (*John*'s) is a "spiritual romance", "a poem not a history", like *Pilgrim's Progress*. Lewis comments:

Note that he regards *Pilgrim's Progress*, a story which professes to be a dream and flaunts its allegorical nature by every single proper name it uses, as the closest parallel... Then turn to John. Read the dialogues: that with the Samaritan woman at the well, or that which follows the healing of the man born blind. Look at its pictures: Jesus (if I may use the word) doodling with his finger in the dust when confronted by the woman caught in adultery; the unforgettable "So, after receiving the morsel, he [Judas] immediately went out; and it was night" (13:30). I have been reading poems, romances, vision-literature, legends, myths all my life. I know what they are like. I know that not one of them is like this. Of this text there are only two possible views. Either this is reportage — though it may no doubt contain errors — pretty close up to the facts; nearly as close as Boswell. Or else, some unknown writer in the second century, without known predecessors or successors, suddenly anticipated the whole technique of modern, novelistic, realistic narrative. If it is untrue, it must be narrative of that kind. The reader who doesn't see this has simply not learned to read. (*Fern-seed and Elephants*, pp. 107-8.)

Pursuing the same argument, Lewis rightly castigates the famous German liberal theologian and 'demythologiser', Bultmann, for his similar blindness to what is plainly revealed about the character of Jesus in the Gospels. Referring to Bultmann's assertion that "the tradition of the earliest Church did not even unconsciously preserve a picture of [Jesus's] personality", and that "Every attempt to reconstruct one remains a play of subjective imagination", Lewis comments scathingly:

> Through what strange process has this learned German gone in order to make himself blind to what all men except him see? What evidence have we that he would recognize a personality if it were there? For it is Bultmann *contra mundum*. If anything whatever is common to all believers, and even to many unbelievers, it is the sense that in the Gospels they have met a personality. There are characters whom we know to be historical but of whom we do not feel that we have any personal knowledge — knowledge by acquaintance; such are Alexander, Attila or William of Orange. There are others who make no claim to historical reality but whom, none the less, we know as we know real people: Falstaff, Uncle Toby, Mr Pickwick. But there are only three characters who, claiming the first sort of reality, also actually have the second. And surely everyone knows who they are: Plato's Socrates, the Jesus of the Gospels, and Boswell's Johnson... So strong is the flavour of the personality, that, even while he says things which, on any other assumption than that of divine Incarnation in the fullest sense, would be appallingly arrogant, yet we — and many unbelievers too — accept him at his own valuation when he says 'I am meek and lowly of heart'. (*Fern-seed and Elephants*, pp. 109-10.)

An example in support of Lewis's reference here to the favourable attitude of many "unbelievers" to Christ, is that of W. H. Lecky, the great nineteenth century rationalist historian, who despite his hostility to the Church (much of it justified) and to certain aspects of Christianity, wrote in his *History of European Morals*:

> It was reserved for Christianity to present to the world an ideal character, which through all the changes of eighteen centuries has inspired

the hearts of men with an impassioned love; has shown itself capable of acting on all ages, nations, temperaments, and conditions; has been not only the highest pattern of virtue, but the strongest incentive to its practice; and has exercised so deep an influence that it may be truly said that the simple record of three short years of active life has done more to regenerate and to soften mankind than all the disquisitions of philosophers and all the exhortations of moralists.

In addition to his literary critique of Bultmann's approach to the New Testament, Lewis rightly draws attention to the vivid and telling eye-witness flavour of some of the most famous passages about Jesus in both John's Gospel and in his epistle. For instance:

> 'We beheld his glory, the glory as of the only begotten of the Father, full of graciousness and reality... which we have looked upon and our hands have handled.' What is gained by trying to evade or dissipate this shattering immediacy of personal contact by talk about 'that significance which the early Church found that it was impelled to attribute to the Master'? This hits us in the face. Not what they were impelled to do but what impelled them. I begin to fear that by *personality* Dr Bultmann means what I should call impersonality: what you'd get in a Dictionary of National Biography article or an obituary or a Victorian *Life and Letters of Yeshua Bar-Yosef* in three volumes with photographs. (*Fern-seed and Elephants,* p.111.)

Having argued that the claim of liberal theologians to be able to read between the lines of the old texts is undermined by their obvious inability to read the lines themselves, Lewis criticises the central assumption behind liberal theology — namely its claim that the real behaviour, purpose, and teaching of Jesus came to be very rapidly misunderstood and misrepresented by His followers, only to be recovered or exhumed by modern scholars:

> ... long before I became interested in theology I had met this kind of theory elsewhere. The tradition of Jowett still dominated the study of ancient philosophy when I was reading Greats. One was brought up to believe that the real meaning of Plato had been misunderstood by Aristotle and wildly travestied by the neo-Platonists, only to be recovered by the moderns. When recovered, it turned out (most fortunately)

that Plato had really all along been an English Hegelian, rather like
T. H. Green... The idea that any man or writer should be opaque to
those who lived in the same culture, spoke the same language, shared
the same habitual imagery and unconscious assumptions, and yet be
transparent to those who have none of these advantages, is in my opinion preposterous. There is an *a priori* improbability in it which almost
no argument and no evidence could counterbalance. (*Fern-seed and
Elephants*, pp. 112-13.)

A similar kind of objection can be levelled at the whole process by which
liberal theologians attempt to reconstruct the genesis of the Gospel texts.
This involves guesses about what vanished documents each author used,
when and where he wrote, with what purposes and under what influences — which in the nature of things are almost certain to be wrong.
Drawing on his own experience of the erroneous views of contemporary
reviewers about the genesis of some of his own writings as well as those
of friends like Tolkien and Roger Lancelyn Green, Lewis argued that
"the 'assured results of modern scholarship', as to the way in which an
old book was written, are 'assured' only because the men who knew the
facts are dead and can't blow the gaff". The conclusion Lewis drew
from his critique of modernist theology, only part of which has been
explored in this chapter, was bleak:

Once the layman was anxious to hide the fact that he believed so much
less than the vicar: he now tends to hide the fact that he believes so
much more. Missionary to the priests of one's own church is an embarrassing role; though I have a horrid feeling that if such mission
work is not soon undertaken the future history of the Church of England is likely to be short. (*Fern-seed and Elephants*, p.125.)

Whether or not Lewis's words turn out to be prophetic (as many fear
today), one thing is abundantly clear to anyone who takes the trouble to
read the whole corpus of his work. His own books and essays probably
offer the best all-round exposition and defence of the Christian faith
written by anyone in the last half century, and as such, represent a unique
resource for Christians interested in meeting the challenge of renewing
the Church and bearing witness to the Gospel in this generation.

4. Political and Cultural Conservative

Any consideration of C.S. Lewis's writings on politics and culture must begin by stressing that he was not primarily a political philosopher, though he did teach political philosophy in his early days as a young Oxford don. But although he wrote very little about these subjects in comparison with his prolific output of books, essays and sermons on central theological themes, his views in these areas are of great relevance and interest. What Lewis had to say about politics and society not only flowed from his understanding of Christianity, but highlighted and illuminated the perennial implications of the Christian revelation for life in this world, and in spelling these out with his characteristic vividness and lucidity, Lewis drew attention to truths whose neglect has blighted the modern world and whose recovery is essential if we are to preserve freedom, excellence and human dignity.

Lewis was a sharp critic of many of the dominant ideological and cultural trends of the twentieth century and to the extent that he saw himself as a lonely and beleaguered spokesman for that central tradition of Christian life and thought which once characterised Western civilisation, Lewis can be properly regarded as a political and cultural conservative in the widest and deepest sense of the word. He was a critic of secular humanism and scientific utopianism, and an opponent of collectivism, egalitarianism and 'progressive' morality, and since this body of ideas and assumptions continues (in various forms) to characterize the mentality of most Western intellectuals, Lewis's critique of them is still relevant today. In addition, Lewis's opposition to theocracy and all attempts to use the power of the State to establish a perfect Christian society, merits close attention, given the rise, since his death, of new theologies which either politicise the Gospel and give it a temporal and socialist slant, or are more theologically orthodox but nevertheless intent on setting up Christ's Kingdom on earth by human efforts, via political institutions and social legislation.

To understand Lewis's political philosophy, or, as he would have rightly seen it, his interpretation of the necessary political and social implications of Christianity, we must begin with a question. What, if Christianity is true, should be our attitude to the world in which we find ourselves? How should we live and what should be our attitude to our fellow human beings and, indeed, to creation in general? Only if we know the answer to this basic question about what should be our inner orientation can we begin to think intelligently about politics and society.

As Lewis perceived, Christianity is neither a world-affirming nor a world-denying religion. It opposes both the secular humanist view that there is no other life except the present one and no goals worth pursuing except our own (mankind's) material comfort and happiness; *and* the view which is implicit in pantheistic religions like Buddhism, that the road to inner wholeness and union with God (or with the soul of the Universe) demands the renunciation of the flesh, including all personal ties and affections, and indeed our very selves — of everything, in short, which differentiates us and binds us to life in this world of suffering and woe. Hence, Lewis points out, the maddeningly double-edged character of the Christian faith as seen from the outside. On the one hand it is a religion which, as a matter of historical fact, preserved such secular civilisation as survived the collapse of the Roman Empire; on the other hand it must be noted:

> ... that the central image in all Christian art was that of a Man slowly dying by torture; that the instrument of His torture was the worldwide symbol of the Faith; that martyrdom was almost the specifically Christian action; that our calendar was as full of fasts as of feasts; that we meditated constantly on the mortality not only of ourselves but of the whole universe; that we were bidden to entrust all our treasure to another world; *(Undeceptions,* p.116.)

To the Christian, Lewis argued, there is no real paradox, since there is no inherent conflict between our allegiance to God and our appreciation and enjoyment of the Universe He created. How could there be? It follows

from the very concept and doctrine of creation that we should both love
and worship our Creator and rejoice in His works, of which we are, in
any case, a part.   Christians may indeed regard themselves, in Lewis's
memorable phrase, as pilgrims passing through the "Shadowlands",
knowing that true life lies ahead, but that does not mean they care any
less than other people about fighting evil and alleviating suffering in this
life. We follow One who stood and wept at the grave of Lazarus, Lewis
pointed out, even though He was about to raise him from the dead,
because death — the punishment of sin — is even more horrible in the
eyes of the Creator, of Life Himself, than in our own. Hence Lewis's
summary of the proper Christian attitude to suffering and death:

> Because Our Lord is risen we know that on one level it is an enemy
> already disarmed; but because we know that the natural level also is
> God's creation we cannot cease to fight against the death which mars
> it, as against all those other blemishes upon it, against pain and pov-
> erty, barbarism and ignorance. Because we love something else more
> than this world we love even this world better than those who know no
> other. *(Undeceptions*, pp. 117-118.)

Christians, then, like all who acknowledge the Moral Law and the objective distinction between good and evil, are called upon to exert every
effort to make this world a better place to live in. But in one respect they
have an even stronger reason than secular humanitarians to 'love their
neighbour' and respect the rights and dignity of every human being.

If Christianity is true, both the prospect of God's judgement in eternity, and the knowledge that individuals are made in the image of God
and have immortal destinies, offer an additional incentive and justification for doing good and fighting evil. At the personal level, Christianity
reminds us, we are confronted by the fact that our fellow human beings
are not only as much God's creation and the objects of His love as we
are, but individuals for whom Christ died. They, like us, have been loved
into existence, offered the gift of redemption and eternal life, and given
that terrible freedom to choose between accepting or rejecting God, between life with their Creator or eternity without Him. They, like us, can
decide whether to be reconnected to the Fountain of Life — the source
of all beauty, goodness and love — or else eventually cut off from Him
for ever, amidst the final and inevitable decay and disintegration of their

minds and personalities. As Lewis once put it with passionate eloquence, in one of his most famous sermons:

> There are no *ordinary* people. You have never talked to a mere mortal. Nations, cultures, arts, civilisations — these are mortal, and their life is to ours as the life of a gnat. But it is immortals whom we joke with, work with, marry, snub, and exploit — immortal horrors or everlasting splendours. This does not mean that we are to be perpetually solemn. We must play. But our merriment must be of that kind (and it is, in fact, the merriest kind) which exists between people who have, from the outset, taken each other seriously — no flippancy, no superiority, no presumption. ('The Weight of Glory', in *Screwtape Proposes A Toast*, p.109.)

Lewis's reference in this passage to the mortality of nations, cultures and civilisations, introduces the other key Christian insight about what should be our attitude to each other — this time in the collective and therefore political realm. And again it follows logically from the Christian view of Man.

Since the individual is God's creation and an object of God's love, dignified with the gifts of reason, conscience, and free will, he does not belong to the State as an animal belongs to a farmer, but has the God-given right to live within a social order which respects his freedom to live his own life and determine his own destiny as long as he in his turn respects the rights of others and honours his obligations to his neighbour. This implies that in the Christian view, the State is not an end in itself like the individual. It is only a means, in a fallen world, to enable people to live together in harmony and in obedience to the Moral Law, so that they can use their talents, develop their relationships, and help each other to know God, enjoy creation and fulfil their potential.

Two other extremely important and related conclusions follow from the Christian view of Man. First, that the primary cause of evil and suffering in the world does not lie in the structures of society or result from any particular set of laws and institutions, but is rooted in our fallen human nature. The wrong laws and institutions may greatly aggravate the human condition, and much of the evil in the world may indeed be due to the behaviour of wicked governments and selfish and corrupt elites, but history as well as common sense tells us that no amount of social and political change, of tearing down and remodelling institutions, has yet succeeded in eradicating selfishness, cruelty, incompetence and tyranny. Old evils may mutate, taking new shapes and forms, but they do not disappear, as the course of all revolutions proves. Hence the implausibility of the socialist and revolutionary claim that suffering, injustice and crime can be removed by the elimination of poverty and inequality.

The recognition of this truth leads to the second conclusion about history and politics: that the nineteenth century notion of the inevitability of human progress is a myth. As the record of our own century has so terribly demonstrated, Man's increasing knowledge and dominion over Nature may have ameliorated the material lot of the human race, but it has also increased the destructiveness and horrors of war, and armed tyrannical governments with new and more potent weapons and instruments of control with which to oppress and manipulate their citizens. And it is at this point that we encounter one of the main themes of Lewis's political writings; his insistence on the dangers and delusions inherent in all forms of utopianism — whether social, scientific or religious.

Human beings, argued Lewis, cannot free themselves in this life from the limitations imposed by their flawed and fallen natures, therefore their attempts to establish a perfect society inevitably backfire and tend to recreate and intensify the evils they were meant to abolish. This happens not only because all schemes of social engineering increase the power of the State — and power corrupts — but also because utopian ideologies typically reject the constraints of traditional morality.

Convinced that they possess the key to history and the secret of happiness, and promising heaven on earth, such ideologies invariably affirm that the ends justify the means and that ordinary moral rules are therefore subordinate to the cause of the revolution, the advancement of science, the survival of the race, the progress of mankind, or whatever the latest utopian shibboleth happens to be. But as Lewis argued in *The Abolition of Man*, and in a cogent wartime essay on 'The Poison of Subjectivism,' there can never be any moral justification for jettisoning the traditional precepts of the Moral Law since the very idea of moral and political progress presupposes a common, objective, and unvarying moral standard, otherwise there is no measuring rod by which to determine whether a particular law, philosophy, attitude or practice represents a moral advance or not. Moreover, the idea that traditional judgements of value can be replaced by a more 'scientific' ethical system based upon supposedly real and solid criteria like the advancement of the species or the survival of the planet, is illusory, because the moral justification for selecting these criteria (e.g. human life is precious, therefore we should love our neighbour and care for posterity) is necessarily derived from the moral code which is supposedly being replaced on the grounds that it is 'out of date'. Hence Lewis rightly concludes that:

> All idea of 'new' or 'scientific' or 'modern' moralities must therefore be dismissed as mere confusion of thought. We have only two alternatives. Either the maxims of traditional morality must be accepted as axioms of practical reason which neither admit nor require argument to support them and not to 'see' which is to have lost human status; or else there are no values at all, that which we mistook for values being 'projections' of irrational emotions. It is perfectly futile, after having dismissed traditional morality with the question, 'Why should we obey it?' then to attempt the reintroduction of value at some later stage in our philosophy. ('The Poison of Subjectivism'; *Christian Reflections*, p.75.)

The belief, then, that modern man can create a new set of values, is a superstition, but it is a superstition with potentially very evil consequences. In particular, it is inimical to freedom:

> Many a popular 'planner' on a democratic platform, many a mild-eyed scientist in a democratic laboratory means, in the last resort, just what the Fascist means. He believes that 'good' means whatever men are conditioned to approve. He believes that it is the function of him and his kind to condition men; to create consciences by eugenics, psychological manipulation of infants, state education and mass propaganda. ('The Poison of Subjectivism'; *Christian Reflections*, p.81.)

Lewis's emphasis on the totalitarian consequences of moral relativism and the logical connection between traditional morality and liberty, is very relevant today, not only because its truth has been demonstrated by the modern world's experience of Communism and Fascism, but because the relativistic mindset of twentieth century humanism also threatens freedom and human dignity in currently free societies — notably in the area of sexual and medical ethics, and in modern 'liberal' attitudes towards crime and punishment.

Although Lewis (given that he died in 1963) never wrote about such matters as abortion, euthanasia, or the use of aborted foetuses in medical research, his treatment of other moral issues, and his general moral outlook, illuminate some of the central dilemmas raised by these developments. Running through his writings on vivisection, modern sexual mores, and crime and punishment, for example, are three related themes: accountability, stewardship and the abuse of power — which apply as much in these areas as in the ones he actually wrote about.

Do animals and unborn babies have rights? Does the advance of science or the pursuit of sexual pleasure or material convenience justify the betrayal of a marriage or the torture of inferior creatures who are nonetheless part of God's creation and capable of suffering and feeling pain? What are the implications of treating crime as if it were a disease, and criminals as if they were patients?

Leaving aside the obvious point, in the case of abortion, that unborn babies are fully human (genetically at conception, and able to feel pain after 12 weeks) and therefore morally entitled to the protection of the law, the main principle underlying the proper Christian response to these questions is the one stressed by Lewis: our God-given human status entails on the one hand that we have the right to life and individual self-determination, and on the other, that we are accountable for our actions, and are under a duty not only to fulfil our obligations to others, but to treat inferiors with kindness. Hence, argued Lewis, we should condemn adultery and avoidable cruelty to animals, and regard crime as a moral offence deserving punishment rather than a psychiatric disorder requiring 'treatment.'

Lewis's discussion of the morality of vivisection is particularly interesting in this context, not only because of its contemporary relevance, but because it so clearly reveals his hatred of cruelty and tyranny, attitudes rooted in his understanding of the Christian conception of Natural Law — with its insistence on Man's responsibility before God for his stewardship of creation.

Even if it is the case that the superiority of man over beast is a revealed truth rather than simply a prejudice in favour of our own species, and therefore conforms to a hierarchical order created by God, it does not follow, argues Lewis, that we have the right to do whatever we like with animals. Their lack of a 'soul'

> ... makes the infliction of pain upon them not easier but harder to justify. For it means that animals cannot deserve pain, nor profit morally by the discipline of pain, nor be recompensed by happiness in another life for suffering in this. Thus all the factors which render pain more tolerable or make it less totally evil in the case of human beings will be lacking in the beasts. 'Soullessness', in so far as it is relevant to the question at all, is an argument against vivisection. (Vivisection, in *Undeceptions*, p.183.)

For Lewis, writing these words in 1947, the victory of vivisection marked "a great advance in the triumph of ruthless non-moral utilitarianism over the old world of ethical law; a triumph in which we, as well as animals, are already the victims..." (*Ibid*, p.186), and one of the areas in which this triumph has become most evident is that of so-called penal reform.

As Lewis explained in a famous and powerful essay on 'The Humanitarian Theory of Punishment,' the modern 'liberal' notion is that it is wrong to punish a man because he deserves it, and as much as he deserves, since this is mere revenge, and revenge is barbarous and immoral. Instead, it is argued, punishment should be regarded as a deterrent to protect society or as a means of reforming the criminal. The central objection to this supposedly 'humanitarian' approach, however, is that it destroys the concept of justice and represents an assault on human dignity and the legitimate rights of offenders.

In the first place, argued Lewis, retribution is the *essence* of justice since it involves the concept of desert. It is morally right that the punishment should fit the crime because a person who knowingly injures another deserves to be treated in a similar fashion and forfeits his right to the freedom which he has abused. Secondly, the very idea of punishment affirms the human dignity of the criminal since it recognises him to be a rational being possessed of free will, and therefore capable of choosing between good and evil and being held responsible for his actions and behaviour. The 'humanitarian' theory, on the other hand, not only separates punishment from justice by rejecting or abandoning this notion of desert; it also treats the criminal as an imbecile or a domestic animal, and paves the way for the creation of a 'reformatory' penal regime under which offenders have no rights but are left entirely at the mercy of 'experts' whose special sciences and techniques lie outside the moral sphere.

To the objection that the humanitarian theory seeks to reform the criminal rather than punish him, and is therefore not vindictive, Lewis retorts:

> ... do not let us be deceived by a name. To be taken without consent from my home and friends; to lose my liberty; to undergo all those assaults on my personality which modern psychotherapy knows how to deliver; to be re-made after some pattern of "normality" hatched in a Viennese laboratory to which I never professed allegiance; to know that this process will never end until either my captors have succeeded or I grown wise enough to cheat them with apparent success — who cares whether this is called Punishment or not? That it includes most of the elements for which any punishment is feared — shame, exile, bondage, and years eaten by the locust — is obvious. Only enormous ill-desert could justify it; but ill-desert is the very conception which the Humanitarian theory has thrown overboard. (The Humanitarian Theory of Punishment; *Undeceptions*, p.241.)

Furthermore, argues Lewis, fallen human nature is bound, sooner or later, to transform the humanitarian theory of punishment into an instrument of tyranny, for if crime is regarded as a disease, it follows that disease can be treated as a crime, and who is to say what state of mind some future government may choose to regard as a 'disease'? In a chillingly prophetic passage, Lewis anticipated, in 1949, the employment by Communist dictatorships of psychiatric methods of torturing Christians and other religious and political dissidents.:

> We know that one school of psychology already regards religion as a neurosis. When this particular neurosis becomes inconvenient to government, what is to hinder government from proceeding to 'cure' it? Such 'cure' will, of course, be compulsory; but under the Humanitarian theory it will not be called by the shocking name of Persecution.

(*Ibid* pp. 243-4.)

Lewis's repeated references to the deadly consequences for civilisation and liberty of false philosophies allied to fallen human nature, is the central theme of all his political thinking. It not only colours his discussion of moral and social issues, but appears explicitly in his writings about democracy and the State.

In opposition to the modern egalitarian view of democracy, which has become dominant since the French Revolution, Lewis emphasized the inherent inequality of man. The case for democracy, in his view, is not that all men and women deserve an equal share in the government of the commonwealth because they are equally wise, which is clearly untrue, but rather that no one is good enough to be allowed irresponsible power over his fellows.

Not only is the wrong kind of egalitarianism (as distinct from equality before the law) a false basis for democracy, and a threat to every form of human excellence — moral, cultural, social and intellectual — but it is also incompatible with freedom, since economic and social differences inevitably arise from the free development and activities of unequally endowed individuals, and therefore cannot be suppressed except by force. That is one of the reasons why revolutionary socialist governments are always tyrannical. In addition, totalitarian rulers have a vested interest in discouraging independent individuals and alternative centres of economic, social and cultural activity, hence their willingness to embrace the forms and rhetoric of egalitarianism and democracy in order to justify their removal of all significant social distinctions. As Lewis's satirical devil, Screwtape, puts it in his speech to the annual dinner of the Tempters' Training College for young devils, in Hell:

> ... is it not pretty to notice how *Democracy* (in the incantatory sense) is now doing for us the work that was once done by the most ancient Dictatorships, and by the same methods? You remember how one of the Greek Dictators (they called them "tyrants" then) sent an envoy to another Dictator to ask his advice about the principles of government. The second Dictator led the envoy into a field of corn, and there he snicked off with his cane the top of every stalk that rose an inch or so above the general level. The moral was plain. Allow no pre-eminence among your subjects. Let no man live who is wiser, or better, or

more famous, or even handsomer than the mass. Cut them all down to a level; all slaves, all ciphers, all nobodies. All equals. Thus Tyrants could practise, in a sense, "democracy". But now "democracy" can do the same work without any other tyranny than her own. No one need now go through the field with a cane. The little stalks will now of themselves bite the tops off the big ones. The big ones are beginning to bite off their own in their desire to Be Like Stalks. (*Screwtape Proposes A Toast,* p.21.)

Lewis's awareness of the perils of egalitarianism and the paramount need to set limits to the power of the State, echoes the views of Conservative and classical liberal thinkers like Burke, the authors of the American Constitution, Acton, Tocqueville and Lecky. But unlike them, he failed to make a proper distinction between liberty and the rule of law on the one hand, and democracy — in the sense of majority rule — on the other, yet the potential conflict between the two haunted Conservatives and Liberals in the nineteenth century and is sadly relevant to postcolonial Africa and the political evolution of many Third World countries.

Although Lewis can be criticised for using the term 'democracy' too loosely and for failing to engage in an explicit discussion of the difference between popular government and liberty, he must have been aware of the distinction since he was alarmed by what he saw as the despotic tendencies of modern democratic states. His anxiety was primarily aroused by the dangers inherent in government economic planning and in the humanitarian desire to use the power of the State to eliminate poverty and guarantee everybody's material welfare from the cradle to the grave. Consequently, whilst accepting the (false) economic arguments for democratic socialism, which he didn't feel qualified to criticise, Lewis warned of their likely political consequences in an article he wrote for the *Observer* in 1958, in answer to the question: "Is man progressing today?"

We must give full weight to the claim that nothing but science, and science globally applied, and therefore unprecedented Government controls, can produce full bellies and medical care for the whole human race: nothing, in short, but a world Welfare State. It is a full admission of these truths which impresses upon me the extreme peril of humanity at present.

We have on the one hand a desperate need; hunger, sickness, and the dread of war. We have, on the other, the conception of something that might meet it; omnicompetent global technocracy. Are not these the ideal opportunity for enslavement? ('Willing Slaves of the Welfare State', *Undeceptions*, p.263.)

Lewis's political Conservatism emerges quite clearly in other passages of his *Observer* article, where he stresses the essential link between private property and freedom, and between economic independence, family life, and personal fulfilment:

I believe a man is happier, and happy in a richer way, if he has 'the freeborn mind'. But I doubt whether he can have this without economic independence, which the new society is abolishing. For economic independence allows an education not controlled by Government; and in adult life it is the man who needs, and asks, nothing of Government who can criticize its acts and snap his fingers at its ideology. Read Montaigne; that's the voice of a man with his legs under his own table, eating the mutton and turnips raised on his own land. Who will talk like that when the State is everyone's schoolmaster and employer? (*Ibid* pp. 263-4.)

Who, surveying the dismal and despotic record of socialism throughout the world, can deny the truth or the prophetic insight of Lewis's words?

Lewis's awareness of fallen man's inevitable tendency to abuse power explains his hostility to socialism, but it is nowhere more evident, or eloquently expressed, than in his opposition to theocracy.

Whilst it might seem right in theory, Lewis argued, that learned priests should govern ignorant laymen, or that a righteous Church should be given absolute control over society, the temptation to accept a theocratic form of government (should it arise) should be resisted. Christians are not only, like everyone else, fallen, and therefore subject to the same tendency to be warped and corrupted by excessive power; they are likely to become even more oppressive tyrants than their irreligious counterparts, since their theocratic despotism is likely to be reinforced by a perverted self-righteousness which would suppress all inner doubts about their own behaviour and silence that voice of self-criticism essential to the correction of all error and injustice:

I am a democrat because I believe that no man or group of men is good enough to be trusted with uncontrolled power over others. And the higher the pretentions of such power, the more dangerous I think it both to the rulers and to the subjects. Hence Theocracy is the worst of all governments. If we must have a tyrant a robber baron is far better than an inquisitor. The baron's cruelty may sometimes sleep, his cupidity at some point be sated; and since he dimly knows he is doing wrong he may possibly repent. But the inquisitor who mistakes his own cruelty and lust for power and fear for the voice of Heaven will torment us infinitely because he torments us with the approval of his own conscience and his better impulses appear to him as temptations. And since Theocracy is the worst, the nearer any government approaches to Theocracy the worse it will be. A metaphysic, held by the rulers with the force of a religion, is a bad sign. It forbids them, like the inquisitor, to admit any grain of truth or good in their opponents, it abrogates the ordinary rules of morality, and it gives a seemingly high, super-personal sanction to all the very ordinary human passions by which, like other men, the rulers will frequently be actuated. In a word, it forbids wholesome doubt. ('A Reply to Professor Haldane', in *Of Other Worlds: Essays and Stories*, p.81.)

One has only to recall the horrors of the Spanish Inquisition in the sixteenth century, the atrocities committed by the Anabaptist rulers of Munster in the same period, or the grim rule of the 'elect' in Calvin's Geneva, to agree with Lewis about the dangers of theocracy. And his words aptly describe the 'atheist Theocracies' of the modern world, in which Lenin's 'Party of the New Type' summons the new god of History to vindicate its violence and wipe its conscience clean.

Lewis's opposition to theocracy and to the use of compulsion and the power of the State in religious matters, is not only expressed in his 'Reply to Professor Haldane' but also surfaces in his encyclopaedic survey of English literature in the sixteenth century, published by Oxford University Press in 1954. There he notes with sadness the degree to which intolerance seemed a universal blind-spot which afflicted Catholics, Calvinists and Anglicans in equal measure, and in deploring this, Lewis has powerful historical as well as philosophical arguments on his side. Quite apart from the moral undesirability of violating freedom of conscience, it can be argued that one of the principal consequences of religious persecution and sectarian hatred during this period was to discredit real Christianity and encourage the growth of an intolerant atheism and anti-clericalism which not only contributed to the Jacobin Terror of the French Revolution, but has gone on to fuel all the totalitarian socialist movements of the twentieth century.

Lewis's detestation of cruelty and tyranny, and his awareness of its ideological and spiritual roots, is the most interesting feature of his political thinking, but underlying it is a moral outlook pervaded by an acute awareness of the difference between goodness and power, merit and success. God, insisted Lewis, should be loved and obeyed because He is loving and good, not because He is omnipotent, since to worship power for its own sake blurs the distinction between good and evil, and is therefore both cowardly and diabolical. That is why, for example, one of the most attractive features for Lewis of Nordic mythology was its noble and heroic rejection of the doctrine that might is right. In a wartime article celebrating the inability of the Nazis to digest the moral content and grandeur of the story of Siegfried in the Nibelungs, especially Wagner's version of it, Lewis commented:

What business have people who call might right to say they are worshippers of Odin? The whole point about Odin was that he had the right but not the might. The whole point about Norse religion was that it alone of all mythologies told men to serve gods who are admittedly fighting with their backs to the wall and would certainly be defeated in the end. 'I am off to die with Odin' said the rover in Stevenson's fable, thus proving that Stevenson understood something about the Nordic spirit which Germany has never been able to understand at all. The gods will fall. The wisdom of Odin, the humorous courage of Thor (Thor was something of a Yorkshireman) and the beauty of Balder will all be smashed eventually by the *realpolitik* of the stupid giants and mis-shapen trolls. But that does not in the least alter the allegiance of any free man. Hence, as we should expect, real Germanic poetry is all about heroic stands, and fighting against hopeless odds. ('First and Second Things', *Undeceptions*, pp. 229-30.)

It was C. S. Lewis's great merit as a thinker, scholar and Christian apologist, that like the heroes of his favourite Nordic myths, he never hesitated in all his writings to swim against the ideological and cultural tide, however dominant and threatening it seemed. That is one of the reasons why his work is of such abiding interest and value.

5. Christian Truth in Lewis's fiction

If versatility is one of the hallmarks of genius, C.S. Lewis certainly deserves the label. As a writer of fiction, an English and Classical scholar, and a Christian apologist, the range of his thought and the extent of his knowledge was extraordinary, but it is as an author of 'children's fantasy' and 'science fiction' that he is best known to the general public. And while it is probably true to say that most readers of his fiction, particularly of the Narnian stories, enjoy his books without detecting or fully grasping their Christian content, it is arguably the case that here more than anywhere else we encounter C.S. Lewis, the 'apostle to the sceptics', in his most attractive and persuasive guise. Time and again Christian truths and perspectives bubble up in the midst of his stories, but always in the most natural and unforced way, for it must again be emphasized that neither the *Chronicles of Narnia* nor his 'science fiction' trilogy were conceived or written with a didactic purpose. As Lewis himself believed, deliberate attempts to build a story around a Christian message usually fail artistically, consequently it is better if it is allowed to emerge of its own accord from an independently inspired narrative. Describing the genesis of his own 'fantasies', Lewis revealed that all his seven Narnian books, and his three science fiction books began with seeing pictures in his head — a faun carrying an umbrella, a queen on a sledge, a magnificent lion. Then came the Form: the fairy tale:

> ... (as Author) I wrote fairy tales because the Fairy Tale seemed the ideal Form for the stuff I had to say.
>
> Then of course the Man in me began to have his turn. I thought I saw how stories of this kind could steal past a certain inhibition which had paralysed much of my own religion in childhood. Why did one find it so hard to feel as one was told one ought to feel about God or

about the sufferings of Christ? I thought the chief reason was that one was told one ought to. An obligation to feel can freeze feelings. And reverence itself did harm. The whole subject was associated with lowered voices; almost as if it were something medical. But supposing that by casting all these things into an imaginary world, stripping them of their stained-glass and Sunday school associations, one could make them for the first time appear in their real potency? Could one not thus steal past those watchful dragons? I thought one could. (*Of Other worlds: Essays and stories*, pp. 42 and 36-7.)

Whether some of the central themes of Christianity manage to "steal past those watchful dragons" and present themselves afresh in Lewis's stories, depends, of course, on the reader, but regardless of whether they do so or not in particular cases, they are certainly present and worth highlighting for anyone interested in Lewis's understanding and presentation of the Christian faith.

How, then, do the *Chronicles of Narnia* and Lewis's science fiction trilogy reflect and express their author's Christian outlook?

It seems to me that they provide striking examples of Lewis's capacity for penetrating to the heart of the Gospel and revealing God's nature and character in fresh but authentic guises. They also reveal an acute awareness of the nature of evil and the process of temptation, as well as exuding an intense and often humorous sympathy for human foibles and weakness.

The seven volumes making up the *Chronicles of Narnia* are ostensibly 'children's' books, but like all the great children's classics of the English language — from *Alice in Wonderland* to *The Wind in the Willows* — they have a timeless appeal that transcends age differences, and adults can enjoy them as much, if not more, than children. The imaginary country they describe — Narnia — is a beautiful world of mountains and lakes, rivers and streams, wooded hills and gently rolling countryside, redolent of the rural England and Ireland in which Lewis loved to walk and climb from earliest boyhood, and this enchanted land is peopled with talking animals (a recurring motif in English literature) ruled by human kings and queens ("Sons of Adam and Daughters of Eve") brought into Narnia from our own world, where they are usually children. In this imaginary country the struggle between good and evil, and the drama of human destiny, is played out from the creation of

Narnia in *The Magician's Nephew* to its (apparent) destruction in *The Last Battle*, and central to its theme is the pivotal character of Aslan the Great Lion, the Christ figure who presides over that world and whose impact on its characters (human and animal) is always the chief ingredient in the unfolding of each separate story.

The Magician's Nephew embraces the themes of the Creation and the Fall, and the choice individuals face between self-centredness and God-centredness, between accepting or rejecting their derived and creaturely status in relation to God. It also describes the nature and consequences of pride and evil in its portrayal of the Witch Queen Jadis (former Empress of Charn), and contrasts it with the Divine goodness and tenderness of Aslan — especially when drawing attention to the contrasting attitudes of these two characters towards power and kingship. The sequel, *The Lion, The Witch, and the Wardrobe,* in which Aslan is sacrificially killed by Jadis (now the 'White Witch') in the place of the erstwhile traitor, Edmund, and is subsequently resurrected, introduces the theme of the Atonement; whilst the last of the Narnian chronicles, *The Last Battle,* is essentially a story about Christ's Second Coming and the Last Judgement — the moral of the tale being the need to resist deception and to be faithful unto death in the battle against evil.

While it must be continually stressed that none of Lewis's Narnia books sets out to preach a Christian message, their Christian content emerging as a natural, organic part of each and every story, their spiritual flavour is unmistakable and leaves the discerning reader with the impression of encountering Something that is both novel and strangely familiar. Christians in particular often find that the character of Aslan and his dealings with the principal actors involved in each story, mirrors their own experience of God. But regardless of how many readers fall into this category, Lewis's Narnian chronicles are a rich quarry of Christian truth and contain numerous passages — of description and dialogue — which convey the character of God, the meaning of the Gospel, and the nature of the human condition, as clearly and vividly as his most learned and lucid apologetic works.

The great truth, for instance, that God is the Creator and as such, the author and source of all that is living and beautiful, is graphically and practically conveyed in the description in *The Magician's Nephew* of Aslan's creation of Narnia — which He sings into existence. Just as the

Book of Genesis records the creation of our universe in response to the detailed commands of God ("God said, 'Let there be light,' and there was light" — *Genesis 1:3*), so Narnia comes into being as the embodiment of the Lion's song — each variation of note and rhythm corresponding to the creation of a different part of the Narnian world.

After vivid and humorous descriptions of Aslan's creation of all the different birds and animals, from the elephants to the frogs, the solemn and beautiful climax is reached as a group of specially chosen animals is gathered in a circle around Aslan:

> The Lion, whose eyes never blinked, stared at the animals as hard as if he was going to burn them up with his mere stare. And gradually a change came over them. The smaller ones — the rabbits, moles and such-like — grew a good deal larger. The very big ones — you noticed it most with the elephants — grew a little smaller. Many animals sat up on their hind legs. Most put their heads on one side as if they were trying very hard to understand. The Lion opened his mouth, but no sound came from it; he was breathing out, a long, warm breath; it seemed to sway all the beasts as the wind sways a line of trees. Far overhead from beyond the veil of blue sky which hid them the stars sang again: a pure, cold, difficult music. Then there came a swift flash like fire (but it burnt nobody) either from the sky or from the Lion itself, and every drop of blood tingled in the children's bodies, and the deepest, wildest voice they had ever heard was saying: 'Narnia, Narnia, Narnia, awake. Love. Think. Speak. Be walking trees. Be talking beasts. Be divine waters.' (*The Magician's Nephew*, pp. 107-8.)

Thus does Lewis convey the Christian and biblical idea of creation as the sovereign and loving act by which God, Who is self-sufficient and self-existent, calls into being that which did not previously exist — reminding us that life is an unmerited gift from Above and that all our dealings with God should therefore be rooted in gratitude and an awareness that we are not autonomous and independent of our Maker.

The creative love of God mirrored in the character of Aslan throws into sharp relief the darkness that reigns in the heart of the dazzlingly beautiful but evil Empress Jadis. She is proud and self-centred, wholly and only concerned with her power, prestige and position, and as a result, she is full of hate for Aslan and totally contemptuous of the lives, happiness and rights of others. Her attitude towards her kingdom and her subjects is consequently that of the tyrant, emphasising once more the intimate link between pride and despotism, self-centredness and cruelty.

The difference between the Christian notion of power and authority and that of Satan and fallen human nature, is brought out explicitly in *The Magician's Nephew* in the passage in which Aslan appoints a London cabby to be the first King of Narnia. It not only reminds us that God is no respecter of persons, choosing and rewarding His servants according to their character rather than their social position, but emphasises the idea that rulers are trustees and stewards, entrusted by God with the responsibility of guarding the rights and liberties of their citizens.

Lewis's creation of Aslan as a credible mythological portrait of Christ is the central achievement of his Narnian tales, not only because of what he makes Aslan say or do, but because his presentation of God as a Lion conveys two great truths about the Incarnation in a single inspired picture: as 'King of the Beasts', the Lion is an effective image of Christ's Kingship and Divinity; as an animal, it is a reminder that the Incarnate God shares our flesh and knows our frailty and sorrows. In addition, the way in which Aslan deals with both the main and peripheral characters in the Narnian stories also reveals Lewis's understanding of God's heart and love, particularly His justice and mercy. The most striking and interesting example of this is the encounter between Aslan and the good Carlomene near the end of *The Last Battle*.

In this passage, which can be read as a parable about judgement and salvation, an enemy of Narnia — a brave and honest Carlomene warrior called Emeth, who is a sincere follower of the wicked Carlomene god, Tash (a demon), believing him to be the only true and holy God, describes his meeting with Aslan in the 'Heaven' of the new Narnia:

> ... the Glorious One bent down his golden head and touched my forehead with his tongue and said, Son, thou art welcome. But I said, Alas, Lord, I am no son of thine but the servant of Tash. He answered, Child, all the service thou has done to Tash, I account as service done to me. Then by reason of my great desire for wisdom and understanding, I overcame my fear and questioned the Glorious One and said, Lord, is it then true, as the Ape said, that thou and Tash are one? The Lion growled so that the earth shook (but his wrath was not against me) and said, It is false. Not because he and I are one, but because we

are opposites, I take to me the services which thou hast done to him. For I and he are of such different kinds that no service which is vile can be done to me, and none which is not vile can be done to him. Therefore if any man swear by Tash and keep his oath for the oath's sake, it is by me that he has truly sworn, though he know it not, and it is I who reward him. And if any man do a cruelty in my name, then, though he says the name Aslan, it is Tash whom he serves and by Tash his deed is accepted. Dost thou understand, Child? I said, Lord, thou knowest how much I understand. But I said also (for the truth constrained me), Yet I have been seeking Tash all my days. Beloved, said the Glorious One, unless thy desire had been for me thou wouldst not have sought so long and so truly. For all find what they truly seek. (*The Last Battle*, pp. 148-9.)

God, in short, does not judge by appearances but looks at the heart of a man, as many passages in the Bible emphasise (e.g. *I Samuel 16:7* and *I Corinthians 4:5*). Aslan accepts the good Carlomene rather than condemning him because He graciously regards Emeth's good deeds and pure (if ignorant) love for Tash as an unconscious act of homage and allegiance to Himself. This does not mean, however, that Lewis is contradicting the Christian affirmation that we are not reconciled to God by "works" but only through Christ. He is not saying, in this passage, that an individual's deeds can be good enough to buy himself a place in Heaven without the atoning sacrifice of Jesus on the Cross. He is simply suggesting that people's acts and attitudes reveal what lies in their hearts, and only God can evaluate their true significance and determine whether they represent 'faith' in the sense of an adequate response to His light on the part of those whose lack of explicit allegiance to Christ is rooted in honest ignorance and misunderstanding.

In *Genesis 18:25* Abraham says to God: "... Shall not the Judge of all the earth do right?" Lewis's story of the good Carlomene's encounter with Aslan expresses his faith in a God who does just that.

Despite the obvious parallels between Aslan and Jesus and the many Christian themes touched upon in *The Chronicles of Narnia*, many people — especially children — can read these stories for their own sake and remain entirely blind to their religious and spiritual significance. Lewis's 'science fiction' trilogy, on the other hand, is much more explicit in its Christian content whilst losing none of that imaginative freshness and originality which is such a striking feature of his excursions into fantasy.

The first two volumes, *Out of the Silent Planet* and *Voyage to Venus* (*Perelandra*) describe the interplanetary travels of a Cambridge philologist called Ransom, and explore two interconnected themes: the significance for Christianity of the possible discovery of other inhabited planets and intelligent species; and the moral and spiritual dangers inherent in what Lewis called the "metabiological heresy", namely the belief "that the supreme moral end is the perpetuation of our own species, and that this is to be pursued even if, in the process of being fitted for survival, our species has to be stripped of all those things for which we value it —of pity, of happiness. and of freedom". ('A Reply to Professor Haldane', *Of Other Worlds: Essays and Stories*, p.77). The setting of the third volume, *That Hideous Strength,* which is more a tale of the supernatural than a science fiction fantasy, is a sleepy English country town, and although Ransom is one of the characters in it, he is not the main one. Furthermore, the central theme of the story is political as much as religious, representing a fictional treatment of Lewis's argument in *The Abolition of Man* that traditional morality — the idea of an eternal and objective Moral Law — cannot be discarded in favour of some new evolutionary ethic, without destroying freedom and humane values. *That Hideous Strength* also explores the corrupting impact on human character and relationships of the desire to belong to an elite inner ring (in Lewis's eyes the most dangerous form of 'worldliness'), as well as attacking the idea of a scientifically planned society, a fashionable socialist nostrum of the 1940s which Lewis,like Hayek, believed was the road to serfdom. For these reasons, it stands somewhat apart from the first two interplanetary adventures of Dr. Ransom and is less coherent and interesting from a purely theological perspective.

The principal theological theme explored in *Out of the Silent Planet,* is the notion that interstellar space may be full of inhabited worlds faithful to God and untainted by sin, our own human race being the only fallen species in the Universe, and for that very reason confined by God to its terrestrial prison — the vast distances of interstellar space being part of God's quarantine precautions to prevent mankind infecting other worlds with sin. *Out of the Silent Planet* also introduces God under the guise of Maleldil, the name by which he is known to the inhabitants of Mars (the planet visited in this story by Ransom), and one of the highlights of the book is the discussion Ransom has with the ruling archangel of Mars about the rumour in the rest of the Universe that Maleldil once visited the Earth (the "Silent Planet") and in some mysterious way wrestled with and conquered its black *Oyarsa* — the fallen archangel ruling our world. Thus does Lewis introduce the idea of the Incarnation and Atonement as seen from the outside — from the fresh and original perspective of sinless beings in other parts of the Universe.

Voyage to Venus, the second volume of Lewis's trilogy, is an even more interesting and original work because it is an astonishingly powerful and perceptive fictional treatment of the Biblical story of the temptation and Fall of Man — but with a difference: in Lewis's story, Ransom is sent by Maleldil to Venus, a newly created and incredibly beautiful world, to avert its threatened Fall and the destruction of its Paradisal innocence and bliss — a task in which he eventually proves successful after a terrible struggle. The core of the book is therefore the description of the process by which Satan, inhabiting the body of an evil scientist called Weston, engages in conversation with the innocent and newly created Queen of Venus (the Eve figure) in order to persuade her to disobey Maleldil's commandment not to live on "the Fixed Land", the rest of the planet consisting of beautiful floating islands on which the three main characters (Weston, the Queen, and Ransom) find themselves during most of the story. Ransom, on the other hand, does all he can to warn the innocent Queen of the peril she is in, and strives to counter the devilish cunning and attractiveness of the Tempter's arguments in the course of a prolonged mental and spiritual battle, surrounded by the extraordinarily beautiful landscape, ocean and fauna of Venus. What is so fascinating about this lengthy dialogue, is the insight it gives us into Lewis's remarkably acute understanding of the fundamental nature of sin and the character and process of temptation that would face sinless innocence in an unfallen world.

In the 'temptation narrative' in *Voyage to Venus*, the key to its outcome is the attitude of the Queen to Maleldil's commandment not to live on the "Fixed Land". Knowing that she loves and reveres Maleldil, her Creator, and her absent husband, the King, and is therefore unwilling either to disobey Maleldil's commandment or take unilateral action without the knowledge and consent of her husband, Satan — through Weston — seeks to persuade her that Maleldil secretly *wants* her to disobey

Him — that He longs for her to be truly independent of Him because He wants to bring into being wills that not only can but *will* resist Him, since he is "weary of seeing nothing but Himself in all that He has made". The Tempter, in short, by subtly distorting the truth that Maleldil (God) gives us the choice of resisting and rejecting Him in order that we may, of our own free will, be joined to Him in love, tries to seduce the Queen into breaking Maleldil's commandment by exploiting her very desire to obey Him. Like the Serpent in the Garden of Eden, Weston's tactic is to sow confusion in the Lady's mind about Maleldil's (God's) intentions and then coax her into becoming self-centred and disobedient by first arousing in her a self-conscious sense of her own independent worth and grandeur. In doing this, he tries to make the Lady forget her creaturely status and the impossibility of life and love separated from her Creator.

> "And will you teach us Death?" said the Lady to Weston's shape, where it stood above her.
>
> "Yes," it said, "it is for this that I came here, that you may have Death in abundance. But you must be very courageous."
>
> "*Courageous*. What is that?"
>
> "It is what makes you swim on a day when the waves are so great and swift that something inside you bids you to stay on land."
>
> "I know. And those are the best days of all for swimming."
>
> "Yes. But to find Death, and with Death the real oldness and the strong beauty and the uttermost branching out, you must plunge into things greater than waves."
>
> "Go on. Your words are like no other words that I have ever heard. They are like the bubble breaking on the Tree. They make me think of — of — I do not know what they make me think of."... (*Voyage to Venus*, p. 104.)

Although, at this stage of the temptation, Ransom manages to persuade the Lady to resist Weston's promptings, the spiritual situation subsequently deteriorates and the battle takes a different turn before victory is finally won. But whereas the Lady is eventually preserved from evil and the future of her planet secured, the soul of the real Weston is forever lost, for Weston's rejection of Maleldil separates him from the source of life and love and truth, and ensures his damnation. In describing the final ruin of Weston and the destruction of his personality, Lewis paints a chillingly accurate picture of the eventual consequences for individuals of turning their backs on God and rebelling against Him:

> But worst of all were those moments when it allowed Weston to come back into its countenance. Then its voice, which was always Weston's voice, would begin a pitiful, hesitant mumbling, "You be very careful, Ransom. I'm down in the bottom of a big black hole. No, I'm not, though. I'm on Perelandra. I can't think very well now, but that doesn't matter, he does all my thinking for me. It'll get quite easy presently. That boy keeps on shutting the windows. That's all right, they've taken off my head and put someone else's on me. I'll soon be all right now. They won't let me see my press cuttings. So then I went and told him that if they didn't want me in the First Fifteen they could jolly well do without me, see. We'll tell that young whelp it's an insult to the examiners to show up this kind of work. What I want to know is why I should pay for a first-class ticket and then be crowded out like this. It's not fair. Not fair. I never meant any harm. Could you take some of this weight off my chest, I don't want all those clothes. Let me alone. Let me alone. It's not fair. It's not fair. What enormous bluebottles. They say you get used to them" — and then it would end in the canine howl. (*Voyage to Venus*, p. 118.)

It was precisely because Lewis was convinced, as this passage demonstrates, that salvation or damnation is the ultimate choice facing every human being, that he exerted every sinew of intellect and imagination to present the truth of the Gospel in ways that could be understood by modern sceptics and unbelievers. Whether his works of theology and fiction can be considered successful in this respect, however, is obviously a matter of personal judgement for every individual reader. What is not in doubt, is that no Christian thinker in recent times has had a greater impact on his own and subsequent generations, as many can testify from their own conversion experiences. But to understand why this is so, readers must turn from this introductory study and read Lewis's books for themselves.

Appendix A — Selected works by and about
C. S. Lewis

Selected works by C. S. Lewis

The Pilgrim's Regress: An Allegorical Apology for Christianity, Reason and Romanticism (London: J.M. Dent, 1933; London: Collins Fount, 1977)

The Allegory of Love: A Study in Medieval Tradition (Oxford: Oxford University Press, 1936)

Out of the Silent Planet (London: John Lane (the Bodley Head), 1938; London: Pan Books, 1952)

The Problem of Pain (London: Geoffrey Bles, 1940; London: Collins Fount, 1977)

The Screwtape Letters (London: Geoffrey Bles, 1942; London: Collins Fount, 1977)

A Preface to Paradise Lost (Oxford: Oxford University Press, 1942, 1960)

Perelandra (London: John Lane (the Bodley Head), 1943); reprinted as *Voyage to Venus (Perelandra)* (London: Pan Books, 1953)

The Abolition of Man (Oxford: Oxford University Press, 1943; London: Geoffrey Bles, 1946; London: Collins Fount, 1978)

That Hideous Strength (London: John Lane (the Bodley Head), 1945; London: Pan Books, 1983)

The Great Divorce: A Dream (London: Geoffrey Bles, 1946; London: Collins Fount, 1977)

Miracles: A Preliminary Study (London: Geoffrey Bles, 1947; London:

Collins Fount, 1977)

The Lion the Witch and the Wardrobe (London: Geoffrey Bles, 1950; London: Collins Lions, 1980)

Prince Caspian: The Return to Narnia (London: Geoffrey Bles, 1951; London: Collins Lions, 1980)

Mere Christianity (London: Geoffrey Bles, 1952; London: Collins Fount, 1977)

The Voyage of the Dawn Treader (London: Geoffrey Bles, 1952; London: Collins Lions, 1980)

The Silver Chair (London: Geoffrey Bles, 1953; London: Collins Lions, 1980)

The Horse and His Boy (London: Geoffrey Bles, 1954; London: Collins Lions, 1980)

English Literature in the Sixteenth Century Excluding Drama (Oxford: Oxford University Press, 1954)

The Magician's Nephew (London: The Bodley Head, 1955; London: Collins Lions, 1980)

Surprised by Joy: The Shape of My Early Life (London: Geoffrey Bles 1955; London: Collins Fount, 1977)

The Last Battle (London: The Bodley Head, 1956; London: Collins Lions, 1980)

Reflections on the Psalms (London: Geoffrey Bles, 1958; London: Collins Fount, 1977)

The Four Loves (London: Geoffrey Bles, 1960; London: Collins Fontana, 1963)

A Grief Observed (London: Faber & Faber, 1961); originally published under the pseudonym N. W. Clerk

Letters to Malcolm: Chiefly on Prayer (London: Geoffrey Bles, 1964); reissued as *Prayer: Letters to Malcolm* (London: Collins Fount, 1977)

The Discarded Image: An Introduction to Medieval and Renaissance Literature (Cambridge: Cambridge University Press, 1964)

Poems, ed. Walter Hooper (London: Geoffrey Bles, 1964)

Screwtape Proposes a Toast and other pieces (London: Fontana, 1965; London: Collins Fount, 1977)

Christian Reflections, ed. Walter Hooper (London: Geoffrey Bles, 1967; London: Collins Fount, 1981)

Fern-Seed and Elephants and Other Essays on Christianity, ed. Walter

Hooper (London: Collins Fontana, 1975)

God in the Dock: Essays on Theology, ed. Walter Hooper (London: Collins Fount, 1979)

Of This and Other Worlds, ed. Walter Hooper (London: Collins, 1982; Collins Fount, 1984)

First and Second Things: Essays on Theology and Ethics, ed. Walter Hooper (London: Collins Fount, 1985)

Present Concerns, ed. Walter Hooper (London: Collins Fount, 1986)

Timeless at Heart, ed. Walter Hooper (London: Collins Fount, 1987)

Selected works about C. S. Lewis

Humphrey Carpenter, *The Inklings: C.S. Lewis, J. R. R. Tolkien, Charles Williams, and their friends* (London: Allen & Unwin, 1978)

James T. Como (ed.), *C.S. Lewis at the Breakfast Table and Other Reminiscences* (London: Collins, 1980)

Jocelyn Gibb (ed.), *Light on C.S. Lewis* (London: Geoffrey Bles, 1965)

Douglas Gilbert and Clyde S. Kilby, *C.S. Lewis: Images of His World* (Grand Rapids, MI: Wm B. Eerdmans, 1973)

Roger Lancelyn Green, *Into Other Worlds. Space-Flight in Fiction from Lucian to Lewis* (London: A. Schuman, 1957)

Roger Lancelyn Green and Walter Hooper, *C.S. Lewis: A Biography* (London: Collins Fount, 1979)

Douglas Gresham, *Lenten Lands* (London: Collins, 1989)

Richard L. Purtill, *C.S. Lewis's Case for the Christian Faith* (San Francisco: Harper & Row, 1981)

Brian Sibley, *Shadowlands: The Story of C.S. Lewis and Joy Davidman* (London: Hodder & Stoughton, 1985)

A. N. Wilson, *C.S. Lewis: A Biography* (London: Collins, 1990)

Dr Andrew Walker and Dr James Patrick (editors), *A Christian For All Christians: Essays in Honour of C. S. Lewis,* Hodder & Stoughton, 1990.

A Note about Biographies

The two standard biographies of C. S. Lewis are the one by Lewis's friends, Roger Lancelyn Green and Walter Hooper, first published in hardback in 1974, and A. N. Wilson's more recent biography of Lewis published in 1990.

Although A.N. Wilson is a brilliant, award-winning biographer, and has written an extremely readable, interesting and sympathetic book about Lewis, his biography is less reliable in some respects than Green and Hooper's. Thus, for example, whilst rightly criticising the tendency in some quarters to make a cult of Lewis, and drawing attention to Lewis's personal foibles and failings, A.N. Wilson shows little appreciation and understanding of Lewis's philosophical and theological work — though some books, like *The Abolition of Man*, are praised, and Wilson remains an admirer (albeit a critical one) of Lewis's scholarly works on English Literature. Unfortunately, however, his own non-Christian and anti-religious bias — in particular, his apparent conviction that religious faith is ultimately emotional and irrational — makes him unsympathetic to Lewis as a Christian apologist and results in him dismissing most of Lewis's popular theological works as glib and shallow, despite the telling fact that they remain enduring best-sellers which have not only influenced (and frequently converted) several generations of readers on both sides of the Atlantic, but are highly regarded by many academic philosophers. In addition, Wilson's interpretation of Lewis's motives in writing the *Chronicles of Narnia* is seriously distorted by his erroneous conviction that Lewis turned to writing children's fiction because of a loss of faith in his ability to sustain a rational defence of Christianity following his supposedly bruising defeat in his famous Oxford Socratic Society debate against the Oxford philosopher, Elizabeth Anscombe. Since the subject of that debate (the self-contradictory character of naturalism) has already been dealt with in chapter 2, it will not be reopened here, but readers interested in an accurate account of this event and its aftermath should read the relevant pages of Green and Hooper's biography and, in particular, the full and comprehensive essay, 'Did C.S. Lewis Lose His Faith?', by American Professor of Philosophy, Richard L. Purtill, in *A Christian For All Christians: Essays In Honour of C.S. Lewis,* edited by Dr Andrew Walker and Dr James Patrick, Hodder & Stoughton, 1990.

Appendix B — Further recommended reading

(1) The philosophical case for the existence of God.

The following books provide a clear exposition and defence of the philosophical arguments for the existence of God:

The Essentials of Theism, by DJB Hawkins, Sheed and Ward, 1949. (Short, readable, aimed at students.)

The Criticism of Experience, by DJB Hawkins, Sheed and Ward, 1945. (good on epistemological issues, containing a stout defence of our ability to obtain objective knowledge of God and the external world.)

He Who Is, by E.L. Mascall, Darton, Longman and Todd, Libra edition, 1966 (one of the clearest and most rigorous statements of the cosmological argument for the existence of God and related issues).

Words And Images, by E.L. Mascall, Darton, Longman and Todd, Libra edition, 1968 (a very clear and effective critique of logical positivism and the false assertion that the concept of God and religious language is meaningless).

No Absent God, by Father Martin C. D'Arcy, Routledge and Kegan Paul, 1962.

Does God Exist?, by Professor A.E. Taylor, Macmillan, 1947 (a very readable discussion of the philosophical issues and the case for God's existence).

'The Vindication of Religion', by Professor A.E. Taylor, a chapter from a book of collected essays by Anglo-Catholic writers entitled, *Essays Catholic And Critical*, SPCK, 1926. (A very good brief survey of the cosmological and moral arguments for the existence of God, and the argument from religious experience.)

The Faith of A Moralist (2 vols.), by Professor A.E. Taylor, Macmillan, 1931 (contains a very comprehensive statement of the moral case for God's existence).

The Moral Argument For Christian Theism, by H.P. Owen, Jonathan Cape, 1965 (very readable, cogent and rigorous development of the moral argument for the existence of God, and contains an excellent discussion of the nature of moral language and moral values).

The Existence of God, by Richard Swinburne, Oxford: Clarendon Press, 1979.

The goodness of God, by John W. Wenham, Inter-Varsity Press, first published in 1974 (an excellent discussion of the moral problems raised by the Bible.)

(2) The debate about God's existence.

Reason and Religious Belief: An Introduction to the Philosophy of Religion, by Michael Peterson, William Hasker, Bruce Reichenbach, David Basinger, Oxford University Press, 1991 (An excellent, readable and very comprehensive survey of the whole debate about the existence of God, the relation between reason and faith, science and religion, the possibility of miracles, religious language, the problem of evil, etc. Aimed especially at students, it is not only rigorous and informative but contains — with each chapter — a useful bibliography of relevant books.)

Does God Exist?: A Believer And An Atheist Debate, Terry Miethe and Anthony Flew, Harper Collins, 1991.

(3) Science and religion, including the debate about evolution.

Christian Theology And Natural Science, E.L. Mascall, Longmans, 1956 (that year's Bampton Lectures) (A comprehensive, erudite but readable survey of issues ranging from evolution to the origins of the Universe and the nature of human consciousness — by an Anglican theologian with degrees in Mathematics, Physics and Philosophy).

Creation and Evolution: When Christians Disagree, edited by Derek Burke, Inter-Varsity Press, 1985 (Christian scientists engage in a many-sided debate about the scientific arguments for and against the theory of evolution).

The Genesis Flood: The Biblical Record and Its Scientific Implications, Whitcomb and Morris, Baker (Michigan, USA), 1979 (23rd printing). (A creationist classic first published in 1961. The authors, a theologian and a scientist, set out to demonstrate the scientific, anthropological and theological grounds for accepting the historicity of the first chapters of *Genesis*. A very interesting and scholarly book whether or not one agrees with its thesis).

Scientific Creationism, edited by Henry M. Morris, Institute of Creation Research, San Diego, 1985 (a collection of essays by American creationist scientists).

Darwin On Trial, by Professor Philip E. Johnson, Regnery Gateway, Washington D.C., 1991 (a very interesting and rigorous critique of the methodological weaknesses and logical difficulties of Darwinism by an American Law Professor at U.C.L.A. (Berkeley) who was former law clerk for Chief Justice Earl Warren of the Supreme Court).

The Facts of Life: Shattering The Myths of Darwinism, by Richard Milton, Corgi Books, 1993 (a scholarly exposition of the scientific arguments and evidence against Darwinism by an agnostic scientific journalist and engineer who is not a creationist but argues that there is currently no credible scientific explanation for the development of life and the appearance of Man on Earth. Milton's book — now a widely reviewed bestseller — also criticises the British scientific establishment for its refusal to give dissenting biologists a hearing in the pages of mainstream scientific journals).

God's Truth: Why a scientist believes the Bible, by Alan Hayward, M.Sc.(Eng.), Ph.D, F.Inst. P, Marshall, Morgan and Scott, 1977 (later edition available).

Reason and Faith: Do modern science and Christian faith really conflict?, by Roger Forster and Paul Marston, Monarch Publications, 1989.
A Test of Time: The Bible — From Myth to History, by David Rohl, Century, 1995.

(4) The truthfulness and historicity of the Gospels.

He Walked Among Us: Evidence for the Historical Jesus, by Josh

McDowell and Bill Wilson, Scripture Press (Bucks, Amersham), 1989 (an excellently argued and well documented exposition of the archeological and manuscript evidence for the reliability of the New Testament).

Who Moved the Stone?, by Frank Morison, Faber Paperbacks, 1975 (first published in 1930). (A famous classic written by a sceptic who set out to disprove the reports in the Gospels of the resurrection of Jesus but became convinced of their truthfulness in the course of his investigations).

Index